Masterbuilt Electric Smoker Cookbook 2021

1001-Day No-Stress, Mouth-Watering Smoker Recipes for Beginners and Advanced Pitmasters

Hiech Kems

© Copyright 2021 Hiech Kems - All Rights Reserved.

In no way is it legal to reproduce, duplicate, or transmit any part of this document by either electronic means or in printed format. Recording of this publication is strictly prohibited, and any storage of this material is not allowed unless with written permission from the publisher. All rights reserved.

The information provided herein is stated to be truthful and consistent, in that any liability, regarding inattention or otherwise, by any usage or abuse of any policies, processes, or directions contained within is the solitary and complete responsibility of the recipient reader. Under no circumstances will any legal liability or blame be held against the publisher for any reparation, damages, or monetary loss due to the information herein, either directly or indirectly.
Respective authors own all copyrights not held by the publisher.

Legal Notice:

This book is copyright protected. This is only for personal use. You cannot amend, distribute, sell, use, quote or paraphrase any part of the content within this book without the consent of the author or copyright owner. Legal action will be pursued if this is breached.

Disclaimer Notice:

Please note the information contained within this document is for educational and entertainment purposes only. Every attempt has been made to provide accurate, up-to-date and reliable, complete information. No warranties of any kind are expressed or implied. Readers acknowledge that the author is not engaging in the rendering of legal, financial, medical or professional advice.

By reading this document, the reader agrees that under no circumstances are we responsible for any losses, direct or indirect, which are incurred as a result of the use of information contained within this document, including, but not limited to, errors, omissions, or inaccuracies.

Table of contents

Introduction 5
Chapter 1: History of Masterbuilt Electric Smoker 6
Chapter 2: How an Electric Smoker Works 7
Chapter 3: Benefits of Smoker 9
Chapter 4: Tips 10
Chapter 5: Poultry 11
    Buffalo Chicken Dip 11
    Seasoned Drumsticks 12
    Spicy Chicken Wings 13
    Rotisserie Chicken 14
    Turkey Breast 15
    Chicken Skewers 16
    Sweet BBQ Wings 17
    Bacon Wrapped Chicken Lollipops . 18
    Whole Turkey 19
    Chicken Caesar Wrap 21
Chapter 6: Fish and Seafood 22
    Cured Salmon 22
    Brined Bass 23
    Marinated Trout 24
    Shrimps 25
    Stuffed Salmon 26
    Whole Snapper 27
    Smoked Red Fish Fillets 28
    Lemon Pepper Tuna 29
    Sweet Salmon 30
    Seasoned Shrimp Skewers 31
Chapter 7: Pork 32
    Smoked Bacon 32
    Smoked Ham with Glaze 33
    Pulled Pork Butt 34
    Stuffed Porchetta 35
    Savory and Sweet Pork Ribs 36
    Smoked Pork Sausage 37
    Smoked Pork Shoulder 39
    Smoked Bologna 40
    Spiced Pork Loin 41
    BBQ Pulled Pork 42
Chapter 8: Beef 43
    Ribeye Steaks 43
    Beef Jerky 44
    Smoked Pastrami 45
    Smoked Hamburgers 46
    Tri-Tip Roast 47
    Smoked Brisket 48
    Beef Meatloaf 49
    Cross-Rib Beef Roast 51
    Jalapeño Cheddar Beef Bombs 53
    Seasoned Chuck Roast 54
Chapter 9: Lamb 55
    BBQ Lamb Chops 55
    Irish-Style Lamb 56
    Lamb Barbacoa 57
    Smoked Lamb Shoulder 58
    Rosemary Lamb Chops 59
    Smoked Rack of Lamb 60
    Smoked Leg of Lamb 62
    Smoked Lamb Lollipops 63
    Smoked Lamb Breast 64
    Boneless Leg of Lamb 65
Chapter 10: Games 66
    Smoked Rabbits 66
    Venison Jerky 67
    Smoked Venison Tenderloin 68
    Boar Shoulder 69

- Smoked Pheasant 70
- Bacon Wrapped Dove 71
- Whole Quail 72
- Smoked Veal 73
- Smoked Duck 74
- Cornish Game Hens 75

Chapter 11: Sides 76
- Smoked Artichokes 76
- Smoked Asparagus and Onion Mix .. 77
- Smoked Guacamole 78
- Smoked Cauliflower 79
- Corn on Cob 80
- Smoked Portobello Mushrooms 81
- Smoked Eggplant and Baba Ghanoush 82
- Smoked Cabbage 83
- Smoked Sweet Onions 84
- Smoked Potatoes 85

Conclusion 86

Introduction

Masterbuilt Electric Smoker Cookbook 2021 for your masterbuilt electric smoker, use this complete guide to smoke all types of meat. An essential cookbook for those who want to smoke meat without needing expert help from others. Offers detailed guidance obtained by years of smoking meat includes clear instructions and step-by-step directions for every recipe.

Known for quality and innovation, Masterbuilt Electric Smoker sets the standard. With a powder-coated steel outer body, Masterbuilt Electric Smoker house comes with four smoking racks that allow ample room for turkey, sausage, chicken, ham, pork, fish, jerky, vegetables, and more.

You've come to the right place. We have 1001-Day No-Stress, Mouth-Watering Smoker Recipes for Beginners and Advanced Pitmasters. All our recipes include directions at least for the Masterbuilt electric smoker which is by far the most popular but we'll try to include directions for other smokers as well.

Chapter1: History of Masterbuilt Electric Smoker

Smoking food is around us since our ancestors were introduced to the power of fire. With time, the smoking method evolved from cooking in open fire or slow cooking, but each method involved trapping flavors of wood into the food. This technique is now used by the smokers that run on propane and charcoal. Recently, a new version of the smoking device has taken smoking enthusiastic by storm – Masterbuilt electric smoker. So, what's new in it?

Masterbuilt electric smoker are not much different from the traditional smoker; they have more fasting heating mechanism that heat wood chips and is energy efficient. Started in 1973, Masterbuilt is not the oldest manufacturer of the electric smoker. Still, they are one of the longer-standing electric smoker brands. It all started as a backyard project of Dawson Mclemore who steadily keep working on the design and mechanism of the smoker which soon turned into a thriving business. Dawson was doing everything to support and provide his family by working at a Tire and Rubber Company, and during that time, he took upon his welding bobby which led to developing his first electric smoker, and it soon turned into the full-time family business. It was all a leap of faith, and this helped them set their priorities into families and hard work. And, true to their mission, Masterbuilt electric smoker product quality products that are built on their hard work and faith and valuing family.

Chapter2: How an Electric Smoker Works

So, you have decided to purchase Masterbuilt electric smoker? Don't worry about its working because this electric smoker is very easy to operate. Here is how you can use your electric smoker step by step.

- Seasoning the smoker: If you are using a new electric smoker, then you need to season it first. The term 'season' for an electric smoker is to burn off residue, oil, and dust from the smoker that could be hanging in it during manufacturing. For seasoning, first, place wood chip pan and water pan without any liquid in the smoker. Then plug in and switch on smoker and heat for 275 degrees F for 3 hours. During the last 1 hour, fill the wood chip pan with chips by half and wait until the smoking time is over. Then turn off the smoker and let cool completely. Now, your smoker is ready to cook your food.

- Prepare your food: Prepare the ingredients and season them as per your recipe. Marinade or brine meat for at least 1 hour or overnight and then proceed with smoking. If an overnight is too much, then at least marinating food for 4 hours to let flavors of marinade fused into your ingredients and ensure awesome flavors after smoking.

- Preheat smoker: If your smoker is cold, switch it on and preheat for maximum 45 minutes before adding food to smoker grill. Add woodchips into the cold smoker, about half at a time, and fill the water pan with liquid, mostly with water. There are a variety of options for woodchips like apple, hickory, mesquite, oak, pecan, peach, and cherry. If needed, insert dripping pan to collect drippings from meat during smoking.

- Set smoking temperature: Set smoker to 225 degrees F, which is a perfect smoking temperature for most of the meat, seafood, and vegetable dishes.

- Add food into smoker: Once the smoker is reached to preheat temperature, add prepared ingredients of the food to the smoker grill directly or use heatproof pan or foil pan to smoker food in it.

- Add more wood chips and water: Make sure you keep a close eye on the smoke. If you feel the smoke is dying, then add more woodchips and water into the smoker. Pull the woodchip loaded and add more woodchips until filled by half. As a result, the temperature will rise, but it will then return to normal level quickly, so you don't have to adjust the temperature using controls.

- Baste the food: Baste food during smoking to enhance its flavors, or you can brush cooking sauce over the food around 45 minutes before smoking.

- Turn off the smoker: When your food is a smoker, remove it from the smoker and let rest for some time before serving. Meanwhile, switch off the smoker and let cool completely.

Chapter 3: Benefits of Smoker

- Average cost: The price of Masterbuilt electric smoker won't break your bank. The average of their smoker is between $100 to $400.

- Simple to operate: Just turn on the smoker, fill with woodchips and water, preheat it, then load the food, set smoking temperature and go on with your business until the smoker is done with cooking. You need to be smoking guru before using Masterbuilt electric smoker.

- Mess-free: Electric smoker is free from cleaning charcoal ash or any other residue and changing propane tank before or after smoking. Moreover, it uses less fuel compared to other electric smokers like propane or charcoal smoker.

- Easy to clean: Masterbuilt electric smoker is made of stainless steel, and therefore, they are easy to clean. The food, especially meat, doesn't stick to smoker grill or its side and it means you will have to do minimal cleaning after your meal is done with smoking.

- Safe: The dangers in Masterbuilt electric smoker are less compared to other electric smokers. In fact, you would be safer using this electric smoker than using any other smoker.

- Study: Masterbuilt electric smoker is very sturdy due to its thick steel legs, which is great for support. You can even set the smoker to cook for overnight without any worry of messing up your food or someone knocking the smoker.

- Digitally controlled: The time and temperature setting of an electric smoker are digitally controlled. Hence, you have absolute control over the cooking temperature. If the temperature rises from the preset setting, the circuit is broken and isn't establish until temperature drops. In this way, you don't have to babysit your food unnecessarily.

- Consume less electricity: Compared to other electric smokers, Masterbuilt electric smoker require less electricity to operate. And, since the electrical source is neutral and clean, it doesn't leave any flavor, only the wood will leave its flavor in the food.

- Durable: Masterbuilt electric smoker is meant for large families to enjoy smoked food. If taken care, Masterbuilt electric smoker should last a long time.

- Responsive customer service: The customer service of masterbuilt is very responsive. They quickly come to help and solve issues.

Chapter 4: Tips

- Choose the right smoker: Before surfing through stores to purchase your smoker, you need to consider a few things that would help you make a finalized decision. This includes information about the model of Masterbuilt smoker, its dimension, price and much more. When you know what you want, it will be very easy for you to but the right smoker.

- Season the smoker: As mentioned in chapter 2, you need to season your new electric smoker before starting smoking food in it. This step will enhance the performance of smoker and flavors in the food.

- Preheat the smoker: Don't do the mistake of loading smoker with food too early. If you want to cook your meal in the smoker to the perfection, then you need to make sure that electric smoker reaches to its preheating temperature that is 225- or 250-degrees F. Monitor the thermostat or thermometer in the smoker to ensure that your smoker reaches to the right temperature. Then, you can place food in the smoker.

- Use the right woodchips: Make sure that you are choosing woodchips for your smoker that give off unhealthy gas as it can harm you and your family. It is recommended to use hardwood chips like mesquite and hickory for smoking food in Masterbuilt electric smoker.

- Use brine for meat: One of the ways to make sure that your meat is flavorful, tenderize, and delicious is soaking it in a brine solution. Prepare brine solution by mixing salt and spices in water, then add meat and let soak for 4 hours or overnight in the refrigerator. Make sure meat is immersed completely in a brine solution.

- Be patient: Smoking food requires lots of time; it can be as little as 2 hours or can take up to 8 hours or more. So, you need to be patient and just take care of heat and temperature, let the smoker do rest of its job. Along with built-in thermometer, you can also insert meat thermometer to accurately measure temperature. You will probably have to experiment a few times, in the beginning, to get to know how food is prepared properly.

- Clean smoker regularly: A cleaned smoker always give the best result. Therefore, make sure you clean grease or leftover oil in the smoker, or else it will go rancid. Also, remember to never leave electric smoker for too long as it will make its cleaning hard. Most of the models of Masterbuilt electric smoker comes with removable parts that make your cleaning job very easy. Use a mixture of water and vinegar for effective cleaning of the smoker and don't use any chemicals.

Chapter5: Poultry

Buffalo Chicken Dip

Servings: 8
Preparation time: 20 minutes
Cooking time: 4 hours

Nutrition Value:

Calories: 153 Cal, Carbs: 2 g, Fat: 11 g, Protein: 9 g, Fiber: 0 g.

Ingredients:

- 8 chicken thighs
- 10 sliced of bacon, cooked and chopped
- 1 ½ teaspoons salt
- 1 teaspoon ground black pepper
- ½ cup chicken rub
- 1 1/2 cups Red Hot sauce
- 1 cup ranch dressing
- 16-ounce cream cheese, softened
- 2 cups grated cheddar cheese, divided

Method:

1. Plug in the smoker, fill its tray with hickory woodchips and water pan halfway through, and place dripping pan above the water pan.
2. Then open the top vent, shut with lid and use temperature settings to preheat smoker at 275 degrees F.
3. In the meantime, season chicken with salt, black pepper, and chicken rub until evenly coated.
4. Place seasoned chicken thighs on smoker rack, insert a meat thermometer, then shut with lid and set the timer to smoke for 2 ½ to 3 hours or more until meat thermometer registers an internal temperature of 165 degrees F.
5. Check vent of smoker every hour and add more woodchips and water to maintain temperature and smoke.
6. Meanwhile, prepare dip and for this, place cream cheese in a bowl, add hot sauce, ranch dressing, and 1 ½ cup cheddar cheese and whisk until smooth.
7. When chicken is done, shred using a fork and add to dip.
8. Add chopped bacon into the dip along with remaining cheddar cheese and stir until well mixed.
9. Spoon dip into a heatproof pan and smoke for 30 to 45 minutes at 275 degrees F.
10. Serve straightaway.

Seasoned Drumsticks

Servings: 12
Preparation time: 20 minutes
Cooking time: 1 hour and 30 minutes

Nutrition Value:

Calories: 400 Cal, Carbs: 2 g, Fat: 20 g, Protein: 47 g, Fiber: 1 g.

Ingredients:

- 12 chicken drumsticks
- 1 ½ teaspoon minced garlic
- 2 teaspoons onion powder
- 2 teaspoons sea salt
- 2 teaspoons ground black pepper
- 1 teaspoon cayenne pepper
- 2 tablespoons paprika
- 2 teaspoons dried thyme
- 1/2 cup olive oil

Method:

1. Plug in the smoker, fill its tray with hickory woodchips and water pan halfway through, and place dripping pan above the water pan.
2. Then open the top vent, shut with lid and use temperature settings to preheat smoker at 220 degrees F.
3. In the meantime, stir together garlic and oil until combined.
4. Place drumsticks on a sheet pan, add garlic-oil mixture and toss until evenly coated.
5. Then stir together remaining spices, sprinkle all over drumsticks until evenly coated and let rest for 10 minutes.
6. Then place chicken on smoker rack, insert meat thermometer, then shut with lid and set the timer to smoke for 1 hour and 30 minutes or more until meat thermometer registers an internal temperature of 165 degrees F.
7. Check vent of smoker every hour and add more woodchips and water to maintain temperature and smoke.
8. Serve straightaway.

Spicy Chicken Wings

Servings: 6
Preparation time: 10 minutes
Cooking time: 1 hour

Nutrition Value:

Calories: 530 Cal, Carbs: 2 g, Fat: 40 g, Protein: 36 g, Fiber: 1 g.

Ingredients:

For Chicken Wings:

- 5 pounds chicken wings
- 1 teaspoon onion powder
- 1 teaspoon garlic powder
- 2 ½ teaspoons sea salt
- ½ teaspoon ground black pepper
- ¼ cup paprika
- 1 ½ teaspoon cayenne pepper
- ½ cup brown sugar

For Dipping Sauce:

- 3 tablespoons minced chives
- ½ teaspoon salt
- ½ teaspoon ground pepper
- 1-pint yogurt
- ¾ cup crumbled blue cheese

Method:

1. Plug in the smoker, fill its tray with hickory woodchips and water pan halfway through, and place dripping pan above the water pan.
2. Then open the top vent, shut with lid and use temperature settings to preheat smoker at 250 degrees F.
3. In the meantime, rinse chicken wings, pat dry and cut off wing tips.
4. Stir together onion powder, garlic powder, salt, black pepper, paprika, cayenne pepper, and sugar until mixed and then rub this spice mixture on all sides of chicken wings until evenly coated.
5. Place chicken wings on smoker rack, insert a meat thermometer, then shut with lid and set the timer to smoke for 1 hour or until meat thermometer register an internal temperature of 165 degrees F.
6. In the meantime, prepare dipping sauce and for this, whisk together all the ingredients for dipping sauce and whisk well until smooth.
7. Serve chicken wings with dipping sauce.

Rotisserie Chicken

Servings: 12
Preparation time: 8 hours and 15 minutes
Cooking time: 2 hours

Nutrition Value:

Calories: 53 Cal, Carbs: 0 g, Fat: 1 g, Protein: 8 g, Fiber: 0 g.

Ingredients:

- 6 pounds whole chicken
- 1 cup lemon pepper seasoning and more as needed
- Water as needed
- 1-gallon bag

Method:

1. Place chicken in the gallon bag, pour in water, and add seasoning.
2. Seal the bag, place in a tray and let soak for 8 hours or overnight in the refrigerator.
3. Then remove chicken from the bag, rinse well, pat dry and season inside-out with lemon pepper seasoning until evenly coated.
4. Plug in the smoker, fill its tray with hickory woodchips and water pan halfway through, and place dripping pan above the water pan.
5. Then open the top vent, shut with lid and use temperature settings to preheat smoker at 250 degrees F.
6. In the meantime, skewer seasoned chicken onto rotisserie grill.
7. Place chicken on smoker rack, insert a meat thermometer into its thickest part, then shut with lid and set the timer to smoke for 2 hours or more until meat thermometer registers an internal temperature of 165 degrees F.
8. Check vent of smoker every hour and add more woodchips and water to maintain temperature and smoke.
9. When done, transfer chicken onto a cutting board, let rest for 15 minutes and then carve to serve.

Turkey Breast

Servings: 8
Preparation time: 5 hours and 10 minutes
Cooking time: 4 hours

Nutrition Value:

Calories: 64 Cal, Carbs: 4.4 g, Fat: 1.7 g, Protein: 7.7 g, Fiber: 0.2 g.

Ingredients:

- 6 pounds bone-in turkey breast
- 1 garlic bulb, cut in half crosswise
- 3/4 cup salt
- 1/2 cup sugar
- 3 thyme sprigs
- 2 rosemary sprigs
- 10 fresh sage leaves
- 64-ounce apple cider
- 1/4 cup apple cider vinegar
- 4 cups ice cubes

Method:

1. Place a large stockpot over medium-high heat, pour in apple cider along with garlic, salt, sugar, thyme, rosemary, sage, and vinegar, stir well and bring to boil.
2. Then reduce heat to medium level and simmer brine for 5 minutes.
3. Remove pot from heat, add ice, stir well and cool for 1 hour.
4. Add turkey breast into the brine, cover the pot and let soak in the refrigerator for 5 hours or overnight.
5. When ready to smoke, plug in the smoker, fill its tray with hickory woodchips and water pan halfway through, and place dripping pan above the water pan.
6. Then open the top vent, shut with lid and use temperature settings to preheat smoker at 250 degrees F.
7. In the meantime, rinse turkey breast and pat dry with paper towels.
8. Place turkey breast on smoker rack, insert a meat thermometer in it, then shut with lid and set the timer to smoke for 4 hours or until meat thermometer register an internal temperature of 165 degrees F.
9. Check vent of smoker every hour and add more woodchips and water to maintain temperature and smoke.
10. When done, cover turkey breast loosely with aluminum foil and let rest for 15 minutes.
11. Then slice turkey breasts and serve.

Chicken Skewers

Servings: 12
Preparation time: 2 hours and 45 minutes
Cooking time: 1 hour and 35 minutes

Nutrition Value:

Calories: 242 Cal, Carbs: 14 g, Fat: 9 g, Protein: 22 g, Fiber: 3 g.

Ingredients:

- 3 pounds boneless chicken breasts
- 1 large green bell pepper, cored
- 16-ounce button mushrooms
- 1 ½ teaspoons minced garlic
- 1 teaspoon ground ginger
- 1 teaspoon ground black pepper
- 1/2 cup honey
- 1/2 cup soy sauce
- 3 tablespoons orange juice
- 6 tablespoons toasted sesame oil

Method:

1. Cut chicken into 1-inch pieces and place in a large bowl.
2. Whisk together garlic, ginger, black pepper, honey, soy sauce, oil, and orange juice until combined and then add to chicken pieces.
3. Stir chicken well until well coated, then cover the bowl and let marinate in the refrigerator for 2 hours.
4. Then remove the bowl from the refrigerator and bring the chicken to room temperature.
5. Meanwhile, soak wooden skewers into warm water.
6. Plug in the smoker, fill its tray with hickory woodchips and water pan halfway through, and place dripping pan above the water pan.
7. Then open the top vent, shut with lid and use temperature settings to preheat smoker at 250 degrees F.
8. Cut bell pepper into 1-inch pieces and slice each mushroom into half.
9. Assemble skewers by threading chicken piece, bell pepper, and mushroom piece in alternate layers.
10. Spoon remaining marinade over chicken skewers and place on smoker rack, insert a meat thermometer, then shut with lid and set the timer to smoke for 1 hour, turning halfway through.
11. Now add more woodchips and water to maintain temperature and smoke, brush remaining marinade over skewers and cook for 20 to 35 minutes or until the internal temperature of chicken reach to 165 degrees F.
12. Serve straightaway.

Sweet BBQ Wings

Servings: 8
Preparation time: 15 minutes
Cooking time: 1 hour and 5 minutes

Nutrition Value:

Calories: 472 Cal, Carbs: 8 g, Fat: 31 g, Protein: 33 g, Fiber: 0 g.

Ingredients:

- 4 pounds chicken wings
- Honey as needed
- ½ cup BBQ rub
- 12-ounce BBQ sauce

Method:

1. Plug in the smoker, fill its tray with apple woodchips and water pan halfway through, and place dripping pan above the water pan.
2. Then open the top vent, shut with lid and use temperature settings to preheat smoker at 275 degrees F.
3. In the meantime, seasoned chicken wings with BBQ rub until evenly coated.
4. Place seasoned chicken wings on smoker rack, 2 pounds per rack, insert a meat thermometer, then shut with lid and set the timer to smoke for 45 minutes.
5. Then transfer chicken wings into a large bowl, add BBQ sauce and toss until evenly coated.
6. Return chicken wings in the smoker, brush with honey and cook for 15 to 20 minutes or until crispy and internal temperature of wings reach to 165 degrees F.
7. Check vent of smoker every hour and add more woodchips and water to maintain temperature and smoke.
8. Serve hot.

Bacon Wrapped Chicken Lollipops

Servings: 24
Preparation time: 20 minutes
Cooking time: 60 minutes

Nutrition Value:

Calories: 212 Cal, Carbs: 4.8 g, Fat: 10.8 g, Protein: 22.8 g, Fiber: 0.6 g.

Ingredients:

- 4 pounds chicken drumsticks
- 2 pounds sliced bacon
- ½ cup sweet barbecue rub
- Honey as needed

Method:

1. Plug in the smoker, fill its tray with hickory woodchips and water pan halfway through, and place dripping pan above the water pan.
2. Then open the top vent, shut with lid and use temperature settings to preheat smoker at 275 degrees F.
3. In the meantime, season chicken with barbecue rub and then wrap with bacon.
4. Place bacon wrapped chicken on smoker rack, drizzle with honey, insert a meat thermometer in it, then shut with lid and set the timer to smoke for 30 to 60 minutes or more until meat thermometer registers an internal temperature of 165 degrees F.
5. Serve straightaway.

Whole Turkey

Servings: 28
Preparation time: 15 minutes
Cooking time: 9 hours and 20 minutes;

Nutrition Value:

Calories: 48.2 Cal, Carbs: 0 g, Fat: 1.4 g, Protein: 8.3 g, Fiber: 0 g.

Ingredients:

- 14-pound whole turkey
- 1 lemon, quartered
- 1 medium apple, quartered
- 1 medium white onion, peeled and half
- 1 teaspoon minced garlic
- 2 teaspoons sea salt
- 1 ½ teaspoon ground black pepper
- 2 teaspoons paprika
- 2 teaspoons dried oregano
- 2 tablespoons dried thyme
- 1 teaspoon dried rosemary
- 1 tablespoon powdered sage
- 3 tablespoons olive oil
- 3 tablespoons unsalted butter, softened
- 1/2 cup apple cider and more as needed
- 1/2 cup water and more as needed

Method:

1. Plug in the smoker, fill its tray with apple woodchips and water pan with water and apple cider half way, and place dripping pan above the water pan.
2. Then open the top vent, shut with lid and use temperature settings to preheat smoker at 225 degrees F.
3. In the meantime, mix together butter and olive oil until creamy.
4. Place garlic in another bowl, add salt, black pepper, paprika, oregano, thyme, rosemary, and sage and stir well until combined.
5. Rub 1/3 of the spice mixture into the cavity of the turkey, then stuff with lemon, apple, and onion and rub the exterior of the turkey with butter and spice mixture.
6. Tuck wings of turkey tightly underneath it, then place it on the middle rack of smoker and insert a meat thermometer in its thigh.
7. Then shut smoker with lid and set the timer to smoke for 30 to 40 minutes per pound until meat thermometer registers an internal temperature of 165 degrees F.
8. Check vent of smoker every hour, add more woodchips, water and cider to maintain temperature and smoke, and check the internal temperature of turkey after 4 hours of smoking and every 45 minutes.

9. When done, transfer turkey to a cutting board, let rest for 20 minutes and then carve to serve.

Chicken Caesar Wrap

Servings: 4
Preparation time: 20 minutes
Cooking time: 1 hour and 30 minutes

Nutrition Value:

Calories: 533 Cal, Carbs: 52.2 g, Fat: 23.2 g, Protein: 31.4 g, Fiber: 4 g.

Ingredients:

- 2 chicken breasts
- 4 large romaine lettuce leaves
- 1 medium tomato, diced
- ½ teaspoon garlic powder
- ¾ teaspoon salt
- ¼ teaspoon ground black pepper
- ¼ cup grated parmesan cheese
- 4 tablespoons Caesar dressing
- 4 large tortillas

Method:

1. Plug in the smoker, fill its tray with hickory woodchips and water pan halfway through, and place dripping pan above the water pan.
2. Then open the top vent, shut with lid and use temperature settings to preheat smoker at 225 degrees F.
3. In the meantime, season chicken breasts with garlic powder, salt, and black pepper until evenly coated.
4. Place seasoned chicken on smoker rack, insert a meat thermometer, then shut with lid and set the timer to smoke for 1 hour and 30 minutes or until meat thermometer registers an internal temperature of 165 degrees F.
5. Check vent of smoker every hour and add more woodchips and water to maintain temperature and smoke.
6. When done, transfer chicken to a cutting board, let rest for 10 minutes and then slice evenly.
7. In the meantime, place romaine lettuce in a bowl, add Caesar dressing and cheese and toss until mixed.
8. Heat tortilla in a skillet pan until warm through and place on a flat surface.
9. Top with lettuce salad, then layer with chicken slices and roll up.
10. Serve straightaway.

Chapter 6: Fish and Seafood

Cured Salmon

Servings: 3
Preparation time: 14 hours and 15 minutes
Cooking time: 6 minutes

Nutrition Value:

Calories: 210 Cal, Carbs: 0 g, Fat: 12.3 g, Protein: 22.5 g, Fiber: 0 g.

Ingredients:

- 1 ½ pound salmon filet, skinless and boneless
- 1 bunch of fresh dill, chopped
- 1/2 of lemon, thinly sliced
- 1/4 cup salt
- 1/4 cup brown sugar
- 2 tablespoons ground black pepper

Method:

1. Stir together salt, black pepper, and sugar and rub this mixture all over the salmon filet.
2. Place seasoned salmon into a shallow baking dish, top with lemon slices and with dill, and wrap top with plastic wrap and then the whole dish.
3. Place this dish into the refrigerator to marinate salmon for 8 to 12 hours.
4. Then remove the dish from the refrigerator, uncover it, rinse fillet well, pat dry and let rest at room temperature for 2 hours.
5. When ready to cook, plug in the smoker, fill its tray with pecan woodchips and water pan halfway through, and place dripping pan above the water pan.
6. Then open the top vent, shut with lid and use temperature settings to preheat smoker at 160 degrees F.
7. Place salmon on smoker rack, insert a meat thermometer, then shut with lid and set the timer to smoke for 3 to 6 hours or until meat thermometer register an internal temperature of 130 degrees F.
8. Check vent of smoker every hour and add more woodchips and water to maintain temperature and smoke.
9. Serve straightaway.

Brined Bass

Servings: 6
Preparation time: 9 hours
Cooking time: 4 hours

Nutrition Value:

Calories: 25 Cal, Carbs: 0 g, Fat: 2 g, Protein: 4 g, Fiber: 0 g.

Ingredients:

- 2 pounds striped bass fillets, gutted and scaled
- 1/3 cup salt
- 1/4 cup brown sugar
- 1 tablespoon ground black pepper
- 2 dried bay leaves
- 2 slices of lemon
- 4 cups filtered water
- 1/2 cup dry white wine

Method:

1. Place a large pot over high heat, pour in water, add salt and sugar and bring the mixture to a low boil or until salt and sugar are dissolved completely.
2. Then remove the pot from heat, cool brine at room temperature and transfer into a large container with a lid.
3. Add lemon slices along with black pepper, bay leaves and wine, stir until mixed, then add bass, pour in more water to cover fillets completely and let soak for 4 to 8 hours in the refrigerator, covering the container.
4. Then remove the bass from brine, rinse well, pat dry with paper towels and let rest for 30 to 45 minutes at room temperature.
5. In the meantime, plug in the smoker, fill its tray with hickory woodchips and water pan halfway through, and place dripping pan above the water pan.
6. Then open the top vent, shut with lid and use temperature settings to preheat smoker at 180 degrees F.
7. Place bass fillets on smoker rack, insert a meat thermometer, then shut with lid and set the timer to smoke for 2 to 4 hours or until meat thermometer registers an internal temperature between 145 to 160 degrees F.
8. Check vent of smoker every hour and add more woodchips and water to maintain temperature and smoke.
9. Serve straightaway.

Marinated Trout

Servings: 8
Preparation time: 7 hours
Cooking time: 3 hours

Nutrition Value:

Calories: 49 Cal, Carbs: 0 g, Fat: 1.2 g, Protein: 8.8 g, Fiber: 0 g.

Ingredients:

- 4 pounds trout fillets
- 1/2 cup salt
- 1/2 cup brown sugar
- 2 quarts water

Method:

1. Pour water in a large container with lid, add salt and sugar and stir until salt and sugar are dissolved completely.
2. Add trout, pour in more water to submerge trout in brine and refrigerate for 4 to 8 hours, covering the container.
3. Then remove trout from brine, rinse well and pat dry with paper towels.
4. Place trout on a cooling rack, skin side down, and cool in the refrigerator for 2 hours or until dried.
5. Then remove trout from the refrigerator and bring to room temperature.
6. In the meantime, plug in the smoker, fill its tray with maple woodchips and water pan halfway through, and place dripping pan above the water pan.
7. Then open the top vent, shut with lid and use temperature settings to preheat smoker at 160 degrees F.
8. In the meantime,
9. Place trout on smoker rack, insert a meat thermometer, then shut with lid and set the timer to smoke for 2 ½ to 3 hours or more until meat thermometer registers an internal temperature of 145 degrees F.
10. Check vent of smoker every hour and add more woodchips and water to maintain temperature and smoke.
11. Serve straightaway.

Shrimps

Servings: 6
Preparation time: 15 minutes
Cooking time: 30 minutes

Nutrition Value:

Calories: 60 Cal, Carbs: 0 g, Fat: 2 g, Protein: 10 g, Fiber: 0 g.

Ingredients:

- 2 pounds shrimp, peeled, deveined and rinsed
- 2 tablespoons lemon juice
- 2 tablespoons chopped parsley
- 2 tablespoons onion powder
- 2 tablespoons garlic powder
- ¼ cup sea salt
- 3 tablespoons paprika
- 3 tablespoons ground black pepper
- 2 teaspoons cayenne pepper
- 2 tablespoons dried thyme
- 2 tablespoons olive oil

Method:

1. Take a large foil pan, grease with oil and then place shrimps in it.
2. Stir together remaining ingredients except for lemon juice and sprinkle this mixture on all over shrimps until evenly coated.
3. Then Plug in the smoker, fill its tray with hickory woodchips and water pan halfway through, and place dripping pan above the water pan.
4. Then open the top vent, shut with lid and use temperature settings to preheat smoker at 250 degrees F.
5. Drizzle 1 tablespoon lemon juice over shrimps, then place the pan on smoker rack, then shut with lid and set the timer to smoke for 30 minutes or until shrimps are opaque, stirring halfway through.
6. When done, remove the pan from the smoker, drizzle remaining lemon juice over shrimps and serve.

Stuffed Salmon

Servings: 2
Preparation time: 10 minutes
Cooking time: 4 hours

Nutrition Value:

Calories: 467 Cal, Carbs: 3.5 g, Fat: 24 g, Protein: 55 g, Fiber: 0.5 g.

Ingredients:

- 5 pounds Salmon
- ¼ cup chopped green onions,
- 1 cup chopped tomato, peeled
- ¼ cup chopped celery
- ½ teaspoon minced garlic
- ¼ teaspoon salt
- ½ teaspoon lemon pepper seasoning
- ¼ cup chopped fresh dill
- 3 tablespoons olive oil
- ½ cup dry bread cubes

Method:

1. Place all the ingredients except for salmon and oil in a bowl and stir until mixed.
2. Brush salmon with oil and then stuff with the prepared mixture.
3. Plug in the smoker, fill its tray with hickory woodchips and water pan halfway through, and place dripping pan above the water pan.
4. Then open the top vent, shut with lid and use temperature settings to preheat smoker at 225 degrees F.
5. Place salmon on a foil pan, then place it on smoker rack, insert a meat thermometer, then shut with lid and set the timer to smoke for 3 to 4 hours or more until meat thermometer registers an internal temperature of 140 degrees F.
6. Check vent of smoker every hour and add more woodchips and water to maintain temperature and smoke.
7. Serve straightaway.

Whole Snapper

Servings: 6
Preparation time: 15 minutes
Cooking time: 4 hours

Nutrition Value:

Calories: 117 Cal, Carbs: 0 g, Fat: 4 g, Protein: 18 g, Fiber: 0 g.

Ingredients:

- 5-pound whole snapper, gutted, scaled and rinsed
- 2 tablespoons butter, soften
- 2 tablespoons olive oil
- ½ of medium fennel bulb, cored and thinly sliced
- ½ of small white onion, peeled and thinly sliced
- 1 whole lemon, thinly sliced
- 1 ½ teaspoons sea salt
- 1 teaspoon ground black pepper

Method:

1. Whisk together butter and oil until combined in a medium bowl, then stir in salt and black pepper until mixed.
2. Then plug in the smoker, fill its tray with hickory woodchips and water pan halfway through, and place dripping pan above the water pan.
3. Then open the top vent, shut with lid and use temperature settings to preheat smoker at 225 degrees F.
4. In the meantime, coat snapper with butter mixture and stuff its cavity with fennel, onion and half of lemon slices.
5. Place stuffed snapper between two sheets of aluminum foil, then turn up the foil edges and place on the smoker rack.
6. Then shut with lid and set the timer to smoke for 3 to 4 hours or more until meat thermometer registers an internal temperature of 145 degrees F.
7. Check vent of smoker every hour and add more woodchips and water to maintain temperature and smoke.
8. Serve straightaway.

Smoked Red Fish Fillets

Servings: 2
Preparation time: 16 hours
Cooking time: 1 hour

Nutrition Value:

Calories: 27 Cal, Carbs: 0 g, Fat: 0.5 g, Protein: 5.3 g, Fiber: 0 g.

Ingredients:

- 2 fillets of redfish with skin, each about 12 ounces
- 1 teaspoon garlic powder
- 1/2 cup salt
- 1 teaspoon ground black pepper
- 1/2 cup brown sugar
- 1 teaspoon dried lemon zest
- 1 lemon, sliced

Method:

1. Stir together garlic powder, salt, black pepper, sugar, and lemon zest until combined.
2. Take a glass baking dish, spread 1/3 of prepared spice mixture in the bottom, then later with one fillet, skin-side down and press lightly.
3. Sprinkle half of remaining spice mixture over the fillet in pan, then top with another filet, flesh-side down and then sprinkle remaining spice mixture on top of it and around the side of fish.
4. Cover the dish with plastic wrap and let marinate in the refrigerator for 8 to 12 hours.
5. Remove marinated fish from the dish, rinse well, and pat dry using paper towels.
6. Return fish into the refrigerator for 2 to 3 hours or until dried and then bring fish to room temperature for 45 minutes.
7. When ready to cook, plug in the smoker, fill its tray with hickory woodchips and water pan halfway through, and place dripping pan above the water pan.
8. Then open the top vent, shut with lid and use temperature settings to preheat smoker at 120 degrees F.
9. Place fish on smoker rack, insert a meat thermometer, then shut with lid and set the timer to smoke for 1 hour or more until meat thermometer registers an internal temperature of 140 degrees F.
10. Check vent of smoker every hour and add more woodchips and water to maintain temperature and smoke.
11. Serve straightaway.

Lemon Pepper Tuna

Servings: 6
Preparation time: 4 hours and 10 minutes
Cooking time: 1 hour

Nutrition Value:

Calories: 275 Cal, Carbs: 0.6 g, Fat: 23 g, Protein: 17 g, Fiber: 0 g.

Ingredients:

- 6 tuna steaks, each about 6 ounces
- 3 tablespoons salt
- 3 tablespoons brown sugar
- 1/4 cup olive oil
- ¼ cup lemon pepper seasoning
- 1 teaspoon minced garlic
- 12 slices of lemon

Method:

1. Season tuna with salt and sugar until evenly coated on all sides, then place in a dish and cover with plastic wrap.
2. Place dish into the refrigerator for 4 hours or overnight, then rinse well and pat dry and coat well with garlic powder, lemon pepper seasoning, and oil.
3. Plug in the smoker, fill its tray with peach woodchips and water pan halfway through, and place dripping pan above the water pan.
4. Then open the top vent, shut with lid and use temperature settings to preheat smoker at 120 degrees F.
5. In the meantime,
6. Place seasoned tuna on smoker rack, insert a meat thermometer, then shut with lid and set the timer to smoke for 1 hour or more until meat thermometer registers an internal temperature of 140 degrees F.
7. Check vent of smoker every hour and add more woodchips and water to maintain temperature and smoke.
8. When done, transfer tuna to a cutting board, let rest for 10 minutes and then serve with lemon slices.

Sweet Salmon

Servings: 4
Preparation time: 46 hours and 10 minutes
Cooking time: 2 hours

Nutrition Value:

Calories: 144 Cal, Carbs: 0.5 g, Fat: 6.5 g, Protein: 21 g, Fiber: 0.5 g.

Ingredients:

- 2 pounds salmon fillets, skin on
- 4 teaspoons salt
- 2 teaspoons ground black pepper
- 2 cups brown sugar
- 1 cup honey
- 2 quarts soy sauce

Method:

1. Run salmon fillets with salt and let marinate in the refrigerator for 12 to 14 hours.
2. Then rinse salmon, pat dry and place in a large container with a lid.
3. Whisk together remaining ingredients, pour the mixture into a container containing salmon and let soak for 24 to 36 hours in the refrigerator, covering with the lid.
4. When ready to cook, plug in the smoker, fill its tray with hickory woodchips and water pan halfway through, and place dripping pan above the water pan.
5. Then open the top vent, shut with lid and use temperature settings to preheat smoker at 160 degrees F.
6. Place salmon on smoker rack, insert a meat thermometer, then shut with lid and set the timer to smoke for 1 to 2 hours or more until meat thermometer registers an internal temperature of 140 degrees F.
7. Check vent of smoker every hour and add more woodchips and water to maintain temperature and smoke.
8. Serve straightaway.

Seasoned Shrimp Skewers

Servings: 4
Preparation time: 10 minutes
Cooking time: 35 minutes

Nutrition Value:

Calories: 168 Cal, Carbs: 2 g, Fat: 11 g, Protein: 14 g, Fiber: 0 g.

Ingredients:

- 1 ½ pound fresh large shrimp, peeled, deveined and rinsed
- 2 tablespoons minced basil
- 2 teaspoons minced garlic
- 1/2 teaspoon sea salt
- 1/2 teaspoon ground black pepper
- 1/3 cup olive oil
- 2 tablespoons lemon juice

Method:

1. Place basil, garlic, salt, black pepper and oil in a large bowl, whisk until well combined, then add shrimps and toss until well coated.
2. Then plug in the smoker, fill its tray with hickory woodchips and water pan with water and white wine halfway through, and place dripping pan above the water pan.
3. Then open the top vent, shut with lid and use temperature settings to preheat smoker at 225 degrees F.
4. In the meantime, thread shrimps on wooden skewers, six shrimps on each skewer.
5. Place shrimp skewers on smoker rack, then shut with lid and set the timer to smoke for 35 minutes or shrimps are opaque.
6. When done, drizzle lemon juice over shrimps and serve.

Chapter 7: Pork

Smoked Bacon

Servings: 10
Preparation time: 96 hours and 30 minutes
Cooking time: 6 hours

Nutrition Value:

Calories: 161 Cal, Carbs: 0.6 g, Fat: 12 g, Protein: 12 g, Fiber: 0 g.

Ingredients:

- 5 pounds pork belly, fat trimmed
- 1 cup salt
- 1 cup brown sugar
- 2 quarts water

Method:

1. Place a large pot over high heat, pour in water, add salt and sugar and bring the mixture simmer or until salt and sugar are dissolved completely.
2. Remove pot from heat, let cool for 30 minutes, then pour the brine into a large container with lid and place pork bell in it.
3. Cover the container and place into the refrigerator for 4 days.
4. Then remove pork from brine, rinse well and pat dry with paper towels.
5. In the meantime, plug in the smoker, fill its tray with hickory woodchips and water pan halfway through, and place dripping pan above the water pan.
6. Then open the top vent, shut with lid and use temperature settings to preheat smoker at 275 degrees F.
7. Place pork on smoker rack, fat side up, insert a meat thermometer, then shut with lid and set the timer to smoke for 5 hours.
8. Check vent of smoker every hour and add more woodchips and water to maintain temperature and smoke.
9. Then transfer pork onto a cutting board, let rest for 15 minutes and cut into 1/8-inch slices.
10. Return pork into the smoker and continue smoking for 1 hour or until cooked through.
11. Serve straightaway.

Smoked Ham with Glaze

Servings: 20
Preparation time: 1 hour and 30 minutes
Cooking time: 4 hours and 30 minutes

Nutrition Value:

Calories: 103 Cal, Carbs: 2.5 g, Fat: 4.7 g, Protein: 12.7 g, Fiber: 0 g.

Ingredients:

- 16 pounds baked ham shoulder, bone-in
- 1/2 cup maple syrup
- 1/2 cup cane sugar
- 2 tablespoons brown mustard
- 1/4 cup sweet apple cider

Method:

1. Rinse ham, pat dry with paper towels, place it on a foil pan and let rest for 45 minutes at room temperature.
2. Then plug in the smoker, fill its tray with apple woodchips and water pan halfway through, and place dripping pan above the water pan.
3. Then open the top vent, shut with lid and use temperature settings to preheat smoker at 250 degrees F.
4. In the meantime, use a sharp knife to score pork about ½ inch deep diamond pattern.
5. Place pork on smoker rack, insert a meat thermometer, then shut with lid and set the timer to smoke for 1 to 1 ½ hour or more until meat thermometer registers an internal temperature of 130 degrees F.
6. Check vent of smoker every hour and add more woodchips and water to maintain temperature and smoke.
7. Meanwhile, prepare the glaze and for this, place a small saucepan over medium heat, add remaining ingredients, stir well and cook for 5 to 10 minutes or until slightly thick.
8. When done, transfer pork onto a cutting board, let cool for 15 minutes and then brush with prepare glaze until evenly coated on all sides.
9. Return ham into the smoker and cook for another 2 to 3 hours or until meat thermometer register an internal temperature of 140 degrees F.
10. Transfer ham to a cutting board, cover with foil, let rest for 15 minutes and then slice to serve.

Pulled Pork Butt

Servings: 12
Preparation time: 12 hours and 10 minutes
Cooking time: 9 hours

Nutrition Value:

Calories: 248 Cal, Carbs: 0 g, Fat: 18 g, Protein: 20 g, Fiber: 0 g.

Ingredients:

- 8-pound pork butt roast, bone-in, and fat trimmed
- 1 tablespoon onion powder
- 1 tablespoon garlic powder
- 3 tablespoons sea salt
- 2 teaspoons ground black pepper
- 1/3 cup brown sugar
- 2 tablespoons paprika
- 1/2 teaspoon cayenne pepper
- 5 tablespoons yellow mustard
- Apple cider vinegar as needed for basting

Method:

1. Trim fat from the roast, rinse well and pat dry with paper towels.
2. Stir together remaining ingredients except for mustard and vinegar, then coat roast with mustard and rub spice mixture all over the roast.
3. Place roast in a disposable pan, cover with aluminum foil and let marinate for 8 to 12 hours in the refrigerator.
4. When ready to smoke, plug in the smoker, fill its tray with apple woodchips and water pan halfway through, and place dripping pan above the water pan.
5. Then open the top vent, shut with lid and use temperature settings to preheat smoker at 225 degrees F.
6. In the meantime, remove the pan from refrigerator, uncover it and take out the roast.
7. Place roast on smoker rack, insert a meat thermometer, then shut with lid and set the timer to smoke for 8 hours or more until meat thermometer registers an internal temperature of 190 degrees F, basting with vinegar every 2 hours.
8. Check vent of smoker every hour and add more woodchips and water to maintain temperature and smoke.
9. Then cover the roast with aluminum foil, return it into the smoker and smoke for 1 hour.
10. When done, transfer roast onto a cutting board, let rest for 30 minutes, then remove its bone and shred with two forks.
11. Serve shredded pork as sliders.

Stuffed Porchetta

Servings: 12
Preparation time: 10 minutes
Cooking time: 20 minutes

Nutrition Value:

Calories: 353 Cal, Carbs: 2 g, Fat: 14 g, Protein: 51 g, Fiber: 1 g.

Ingredients:

- 6 pounds pork belly, fat trimmed
- 12-ounce sundried tomato spread
- 2 cups giardiniera, Chicago styled
- 1 cup bacon jam
- ½ cup dry rub

Method:

1. Plug in the smoker, fill its tray with oak woodchips and water pan halfway through, and place dripping pan above the water pan.
2. Then open the top vent, shut with lid and use temperature settings to preheat smoker at 275 degrees F.
3. In the meantime, rinse pork, pat dry and then season with dry rub on all sides until evenly coated.
4. Place seasoned pork on a cutting board or clean working space; spread tomato spread on top, layer with giardiniera and tomato spread, then roll pork and tie with kitchen twines.
5. Place stuffed pork on smoker rack, insert a meat thermometer, then shut with lid and set the timer to smoke for 2 to 3 hours or more until meat thermometer registers an internal temperature of 195 degrees F.
6. Check vent of smoker every hour and add more woodchips and water to maintain temperature and smoke.
7. When done, transfer porchetta to a cutting board, let rest for 15 minutes and then slice to serve.

Savory and Sweet Pork Ribs

Servings: 8
Preparation time: 45 minutes
Cooking time: 4 hours and 30 minutes

Nutrition Value:

Calories: 126 Cal, Carbs: 0 g, Fat: 11 g, Protein: 7.3 g, Fiber: 0 g.

Ingredients:

- 2 racks baby back ribs, each about 2 pounds
- 1/2 cup brown sugar
- 1/4 cup smoked paprika
- 1 ½ tablespoon salt
- 1 tablespoon ground black pepper
- 2 teaspoons garlic powder
- 2 teaspoons onion powder
- ½ teaspoon red chili powder
- Apple cider vinegar as needed for basting

Method:

1. Use a paring knife to peel and remove the membrane from ribs, rinse well and pat dry with paper towels.
2. Stir together all the ingredients except for the vinegar, then rub this mixture on all sides of ribs and let rest at room temperature for 30 minutes.
3. When ready to cook, plug in the smoker, fill its tray with hickory woodchips and water pan halfway through, and place dripping pan above the water pan.
4. Then open the top vent, shut with lid and use temperature settings to preheat smoker at 250 degrees F.
5. Place seasoned ribs on smoker rack, insert a meat thermometer, then shut with lid and set the timer to smoke for 3 hours.
6. Check vent of smoker every hour and add more woodchips and water to maintain temperature and smoke.
7. After 3 hours of smoking, baste ribs with vinegar, wrap them completely in aluminum foil and continue smoking for 1 to 1 ½ hour or until meat thermometer registers an internal temperature of 160 degrees F.
8. Serve straightaway.

Smoked Pork Sausage

Servings: 6
Preparation time: 29 hours
Cooking time: 3 hours

Nutrition Value:

Calories: 265 Cal, Carbs: 1.43 g, Fat: 21.5 g, Protein: 15.1 g, Fiber: 0 g.

Ingredients:

- 2 pounds pork butt, cubed
- 1/2-pound pork fat, cubed
- 1/2 teaspoon onion powder
- 1/2 teaspoon garlic powder
- 1 tablespoon sea salt
- 1 1/2 teaspoons ground black pepper
- 1 teaspoon brown sugar
- 1/4 teaspoon cayenne pepper
- 1 1/2 teaspoons dried oregano
- 1/4 cup water

Method:

1. Take hog casings, place them in a large bowl, pour in water, and let soak for 1 hour.
2. Meanwhile, place pork butt and fat in a food processor, process until grind and place in a large bowl.
3. Season with onion powder, garlic powder, salt, black pepper, sugar, cayenne pepper and oregano, and mix until well combined, set aside in refrigerator until required.
4. Rinse hog casings, then working on one casing at a time, tie one end of the casing and another open end over the nozzle and slowly push meat mixture into the casing until filled.
5. Don't overstuff the casing and once it is filled, tie the other end as well and then tie sausage roll every 4 inches by twisting the basing.
6. Air dry the casing for 1 to 3 hours or rotate casing on paper towel often to dry its surfaces.
7. Then take a large container, layer its bottom with some paper towels, then top with sausage, add more paper towels and then more sausage until container is full.
8. Cover container with lid and place in the refrigerator for 12 to 24 hours or until chilled.
9. When ready to cook, place chilled sausage for 20 to 30 minutes or until their temperature reach room temperature.
10. Meanwhile, plug in the smoker, fill its tray with hickory woodchips and water pan halfway through, and place dripping pan above the water pan.

11. Then open the top vent, shut with lid and use temperature settings to preheat smoker at 250 degrees F.
12. In the meantime, cut sausage at the twisted sections and remove their ties.
13. Place sausage on smoker rack, insert a meat thermometer, then shut with lid and set the timer to smoke for 3 hours or more until meat thermometer registers an internal temperature of 165 degrees F.
14. Check vent of smoker every hour and add more woodchips and water to maintain temperature and smoke.
15. Serve straightaway.

Smoked Pork Shoulder

Servings: 12
Preparation time: 9 hours and 15 minutes
Cooking time: 8 hours

Nutrition Value:

Calories: 343 Cal, Carbs: 0.8 g, Fat: 23.9 g, Protein: 33.3 g, Fiber: 0 g.

Ingredients:

- 8-pound pork shoulder roast, bone-in, and fat trimmed
- 2 teaspoons onion powder
- 2 teaspoons garlic powder
- 2 teaspoons celery salt
- 4 teaspoons salt
- 2 teaspoons ground black pepper
- 1/4 cup brown sugar
- 1/2 teaspoon cayenne pepper
- 1/2 cup paprika
- 2 teaspoons dry mustard

Method:

1. Rinse pork shoulder, pat dry completely with paper towels and place roast in a foil pan.
2. Stir together remaining ingredients until mixed and then season roast with the spice mixture until evenly coated.
3. Cover pan tightly with plastic wrap and let marinate in the refrigerator for 8 hours.
4. Then remove pork from refrigerator and let rest for 1 hour at room temperature.
5. Meanwhile, plug in the smoker, fill its tray with hickory woodchips and water pan halfway through, and place dripping pan above the water pan.
6. Then open the top vent, shut with lid and use temperature settings to preheat smoker at 225 degrees F.
7. Place pork on smoker rack, insert a meat thermometer, then shut with lid and set the timer to smoke for 8 hours or more until meat thermometer registers an internal temperature of 190 degrees F.
8. Check vent of smoker every hour and add more woodchips and water to maintain temperature and smoke.
9. When done, transfer pork to a cutting board, cover with aluminum foil and let rest for 30 minutes.
10. Then remove bone from the pork, slice thinly and serve.

Smoked Bologna

Servings: 12
Preparation time: 30 minutes
Cooking time: 4 hours

Nutrition Value:

Calories: 90 Cal, Carbs: 3 g, Fat: 9 g, Protein: 6 g, Fiber: 0 g.

Ingredients:

- 3 pounds bologna roll
- 2 tablespoons ground black pepper
- 3/4 cup brown sugar
- 1/4 cup yellow mustard

Method:

1. Plug in the smoker, fill its tray with apple woodchips and water pan halfway through, and place dripping pan above the water pan.
2. Then open the top vent, shut with lid and use temperature settings to preheat smoker at 225 degrees F.
3. In the meantime, score bologna with ¼ inch deep diamond pattern, then coats with mustard and season with black pepper and sugar.
4. Place bologna on smoker rack, insert a meat thermometer, then shut with lid and set the timer to smoke for 3 to 4 hours.
5. Check vent of smoker every hour and add more woodchips and water to maintain temperature and smoke.
6. When done, transfer bologna to a cutting board, let cool for 15 minutes and then cut into ½ inch thick slices.
7. Serve bologna slices as sandwiches.

Spiced Pork Loin

Servings: 12
Preparation time: 1 hour and 45 minutes
Cooking time: 3 hours

Nutrition Value:

Calories: 169 Cal, Carbs: 2.7 g, Fat: 5.7 g, Protein: 25.5 g, Fiber: 0.5 g.

Ingredients:

- 6-pound pork loin, boneless
- 1/2 teaspoon garlic powder
- 2 teaspoons sea salt
- 1 teaspoon ground black pepper
- 1 tablespoon Chinese five spice powder
- 2 tablespoons olive oil

Method:

1. Rinse pork, pat dry with paper towels and place on a foil pan.
2. Stir together remaining ingredients until smooth paste form, then rub this paste on all sides of pork and let marinate for 60 minutes at room temperature.
3. Meanwhile, plug in the smoker, fill its tray with oak woodchips and water pan halfway through, and place dripping pan above the water pan.
4. Then open the top vent, shut with lid and use temperature settings to preheat smoker at 225 degrees F.
5. Place pork on smoker rack, insert a meat thermometer, then shut with lid and set the timer to smoke for 3 hours or more until meat thermometer registers an internal temperature of 155 degrees F.
6. Check vent of smoker every hour and add more woodchips and water to maintain temperature and smoke.
7. When done, transfer pork to a cutting board, cover with aluminum foil, and let rest for 30 minutes.
8. When done, transfer pork to a cutting board, cover with aluminum foil, and let rest for 30 minutes.
9. Slice pork into ½ inch thick pieces and serve.

BBQ Pulled Pork

Servings: 16
Preparation time: 12 hours and 20 minutes
Cooking time: 8 hours

Nutrition Value:

Calories: 236 Cal, Carbs: 2 g, Fat: 11 g, Protein: 30 g, Fiber: 2 g.

Ingredients:

- 8-pound pork butt roast, fat trimmed
- 2 tablespoons onion powder
- 2 tablespoons garlic powder
- 1/4 cup sea salt
- 1/2 cup brown sugar
- 1 tablespoon ground black pepper
- 1 tablespoon paprika
- 1 tablespoon dried thyme
- 1 tablespoon dried oregano
- 6 tablespoons yellow mustard
- BBQ sauce for serving
- Burger rolls for serving

Method:

1. Rinse pork, pat dry and then rub with mustard.
2. Stir together remaining ingredients and sprinkle the spice mixture all over the pork until evenly coated.
3. Transfer pork roast into a foil pan, fat-side up, cover with plastic wrap and let marinate in the refrigerator for 8 to 12 hours.
4. Then remove pork from the pan and let rest at room temperature for 30 minutes.
5. In the meantime, plug in the smoker, fill its tray with hickory woodchips and water pan halfway through, and place dripping pan above the water pan.
6. Then open the top vent, shut with lid and use temperature settings to preheat smoker at 225 degrees F.
7. Place pork on smoker rack, insert a meat thermometer, then shut with lid and set the timer to smoke for 8 hours or more until meat thermometer registers an internal temperature of 190 degrees F.
8. Check vent of smoker every hour and add more woodchips and water to maintain temperature and smoke.
9. When done, transfer pork to a cutting board, let rest for 20 minutes and then shred with two forks.
10. Evenly divide shredded pork on buns, top with BBQ sauce and serve.

Chapter 8: Beef

Ribeye Steaks

Servings: 4
Preparation time: 20 minutes
Cooking time: 45 minutes

Nutrition Value:

Calories: 230 Cal, Carbs: 0 g, Fat: 16 g, Protein: 21 g, Fiber: 0 g.

Ingredients:

- 4 ribeye steaks, each about 1 ½ thick
- 1 ½ teaspoon garlic powder
- 2 teaspoons salt
- 2 teaspoon ground black pepper
- 1 teaspoon onion powder
- 4 tablespoons olive oil

Method:

1. Rinse steak, pat dry with paper towels, then brush with oil and season well with garlic powder, onion powder, salt, and black pepper.
2. Then plug in the smoker, fill its tray with cherry woodchips and water pan halfway through, and place dripping pan above the water pan.
3. Then open the top vent, shut with lid and use temperature settings to preheat smoker at 220 degrees F.
4. Place seasoned steaks on smoker rack, insert a meat thermometer, then shut with lid and set the timer to smoke for 45 minutes or more until meat thermometer registers an internal temperature between 125 to 145 degrees F.
5. When done, transfer steak to a cutting board, cover with aluminum foil and let rest for 10 minutes.
6. Slice and serve.

Beef Jerky

Servings: 6
Preparation time: 8 hours and 40 minutes
Cooking time: 3 hours and 30 minutes

Nutrition Value:

Calories: 42 Cal, Carbs: 0.8 g, Fat: 0.5 g, Protein: 8.7 g, Fiber: 0 g.

Ingredients:

- 1-pound London broil, fat trimmed
- 1 teaspoon onion powder
- 1 tablespoon ground black pepper
- 2 tablespoons brown sugar
- 1 teaspoon garlic powder
- 2 tablespoons sea salt
- 2 tablespoons blackstrap molasses
- ¾ cup apple cider vinegar
- 12-ounce dark beer

Method:

1. Freeze London broil for 30 minutes and then cut into 1/4-inch thick strips.
2. In the meantime, prepare marinade and for this, pour in 6-ounce beer in a bowl, add remaining ingredients and stir until well combined.
3. Place broil strips into a baking dish, pour in prepared marinade, toss until evenly coated, then cover dish and let marinate in the refrigerator for 8 hours.
4. Then plug in the smoker, fill its tray with hickory woodchips and water pan with water and remaining beer, and place dripping pan above the water pan.
5. Then open the top vent, shut with lid and use temperature settings to preheat smoker at 180 degrees F.
6. In the meantime, rinse broil strips and pat dry with paper towels.
7. Place loin strips on smoker rack, then shut with lid and set the timer to smoke for 3 ½ hours or until done.
8. Check vent of smoker every hour and add more woodchips and water to maintain temperature and smoke.
9. When done, let beef jerky cool completely on a wire rack and then serve.

Smoked Pastrami

Servings: 8
Preparation time: 8 hours and 20 minutes
Cooking time: 8 hours

Nutrition Value:

Calories: 70 Cal, Carbs: 1 g, Fat: 2.5 g, Protein: 10 g, Fiber: 0 g.

Ingredients:

- 4 pounds corned Beef
- 2 tablespoons Italian seasoning
- Corned beef seasoning packet
- 3 tablespoons mustard paste
- Water as needed

Method:

1. Place beef in a large container with lid, pour in water to cover it, then cover with a lid and let soak in the refrigerator for 8 hours.
2. Then plug in the smoker, fill its tray with hickory woodchips and water pan halfway through, and place dripping pan above the water pan.
3. Then open the top vent, shut with lid and use temperature settings to preheat smoker at 235 degrees F.
4. In the meantime, remove beef from water, pat dry, then coat with mustard and season with Italian seasoning and corned beef seasoning.
5. Place seasoned beef on smoker rack, place meat thermometer, then shut with lid and set the timer to smoke for 6 to 8 hours or until meat thermometer register an internal temperature of 200 degrees F.
6. Check vent of smoker every hour and add more woodchips and water to maintain temperature and smoke.
7. Serve straightaway.

Smoked Hamburgers

Servings: 6
Preparation time: 15 minutes
Cooking time: 1 hour and 30 minutes

Nutrition Value:

Calories: 1046 Cal, Carbs: 31 g, Fat: 8 g, Protein: 13 g, Fiber: 3 g.

Ingredients:

- 2 pounds ground beef
- 2 teaspoons sea salt
- 1 ½ teaspoon ground black pepper
- 6 slices of American cheese
- 6 burger rolls, halved

Method:

1. Plug in the smoker, fill its tray with hickory woodchips and water pan halfway through, and place dripping pan above the water pan.
2. Then open the top vent, shut with lid and use temperature settings to preheat smoker at 225 degrees F.
3. In the meantime, place ground beef into a large bowl, season with salt and black pepper and then shape mixture into 6 patties, each about 6-ounce.
4. Place patties on smoker rack, insert a meat thermometer, then shut with lid and set the timer to smoke for 1 to 1 ½ hour or more until meat thermometer registers an internal temperature of 160 degrees F.
5. Check vent of smoker every hour and add more woodchips and water to maintain temperature and smoke.
6. Then top each patty with a slice of cheese and continue smoking for 15 minutes or until cheese melts.
7. Serve patties in burger rolls.

Tri-Tip Roast

Servings: 6
Preparation time: 1 hour and 10 minutes
Cooking time: 2 hours

Nutrition Value:

Calories: 140 Cal, Carbs: 0 g, Fat: 5 g, Protein: 24 g, Fiber: 0 g.

Ingredients:

- 3-pound tri-tip roast
- 1 teaspoon onion powder
- 1 teaspoon ground black pepper
- 1 teaspoon brown sugar
- 1/2 teaspoon garlic powder
- 2 teaspoons sea salt
- 1 ½ teaspoon red chili powder
- 1 teaspoon espresso powder

Method:

1. Rinse roast, pat dry using paper towels and then score about ¼ inch deep diamond pattern on it.
2. Stir together remaining ingredients, then rub on all sides of roast until evenly coated and let marinate for 1 hour at room temperature.
3. Then plug in the smoker, fill its tray with hickory woodchips and water pan halfway through, and place dripping pan above the water pan.
4. Then open the top vent, shut with lid and use temperature settings to preheat smoker at 225 degrees F.
5. Place roast on smoker rack, fat-side up, insert a meat thermometer, then shut with lid and set the timer to smoke for 2 hours or more until meat thermometer registers an internal temperature of 130 degrees F.
6. Check vent of smoker every hour and add more woodchips and water to maintain temperature and smoke.
7. When done, transfer roast to a cutting board, cover with aluminum foil and let rest for 20 minutes.
8. Slice roast into ½ inch thick pieces and serve.

Smoked Brisket

Servings: 25
Preparation time: 55 minutes
Cooking time: 10 hours

Nutrition Value:

Calories: 71 Cal, Carbs: 0 g, Fat: 5 g, Protein: 5 g, Fiber: 0 g.

Ingredients:

- 12-pound brisket, fat trimmed
- 2 tablespoons garlic powder
- 6 tablespoons salt
- 4 tablespoons ground black pepper
- ½ cup brown sugar
- ½ cup smoked paprika
- 6 tablespoons red chili powder
- 2 teaspoons cayenne pepper
- 2 tablespoons ground coriander
- 4 tablespoons ground cumin
- 2 tablespoons dried oregano

Method:

1. Rinse brisket and pat dry using paper towels.
2. Stir together remaining ingredients, rub this mixture on all sides of brisket, then cover with plastic wrap and let marinate in the refrigerator for 30 minutes.
3. Then Plug in the smoker, fill its tray with mesquite woodchips and water pan halfway through, and place dripping pan above the water pan.
4. Open the top vent, shut with lid and use temperature settings to preheat smoker at 225 degrees F.
5. In the meantime, remove the brisket from the refrigerator, uncover it and let rest at room temperature.
6. Place brisket on smoker rack, insert a meat thermometer, then shut with lid and set the timer to smoke for 10 hours or more until meat thermometer registers an internal temperature of 190 degrees F.
7. Check vent of smoker every hour and add more woodchips and water to maintain temperature and smoke.
8. When done, transfer brisket to a cutting board, cover with aluminum foil for 15 minutes, and then slice to serve.

Beef Meatloaf

Servings: 8
Preparation time: 45 minutes
Cooking time: 3 hours

Nutrition Value:

Calories: 331 Cal, Carbs: 14 g, Fat: 18 g, Protein: 27 g, Fiber: 1.2 g.

Ingredients:

- 2 pounds ground chuck
- 2 medium white onions, peeled and minced
- 2 teaspoons sea salt
- 1 teaspoon ground black pepper
- 1 ½ teaspoon Italian seasoning
- 1/2 cup Panko bread crumbs
- 2 tablespoons Worcestershire sauce
- 1 tablespoon tomato paste
- 1 tablespoon olive oil
- 2 eggs, beaten
- 1/3 cup chicken broth

For Glaze:

- 2 tablespoons brown sugar
- 2 tablespoons yellow mustard
- 1/2 cup tomato ketchup

Method:

1. Place beef in a large bowl and let rest at room temperature for 30 minutes.
2. Meanwhile, plug in the smoker, fill its tray with hickory woodchips and water pan halfway through, and place dripping pan above the water pan.
3. Then open the top vent, shut with lid and use temperature settings to preheat smoker at 225 degrees F.
4. In the meantime, place a skillet pan over medium-low heat, add oil and when hot, add onion, season with salt, black pepper, and Italian seasoning and cook for 6 minutes or until onions are tender.
5. When done, remove the pan from heat, cool for 10 minutes and then stir in Worcestershire sauce, tomato paste and chicken broth or until combined.
6. Add this mixture into the beef along with eggs and breadcrumbs and stir until well combined, don't over mix.
7. Shape beef into a meatloaf, then place on smoker rack, insert a meat thermometer, then shut with lid and set the timer to smoke for 3 hours or more until meat thermometer registers an internal temperature of 160 degrees F.

8. Check vent of smoker every hour and add more woodchips and water to maintain temperature and smoke.
9. While beef is smoking, whisk together all the ingredients for the glaze and brush it on meatloaf after 2 hours of smoking time.
10. Slice and serve.

Cross-Rib Beef Roast

Servings: 6
Preparation time: 1 hour and 10 minutes
Cooking time: 4 hours

Nutrition Value:

Calories: 257 Cal, Carbs: 0 g, Fat: 16 g, Protein: 26 g, Fiber: 0 g.

Ingredients:

- ¼ cup olive oil
- 3 pounds cross-rib beef roast, boneless and fat trimmed

For Rub:

- 3 teaspoons garlic powder
- 1 ½ tablespoon salt
- 1 tablespoon ground black pepper
- 1 tablespoon paprika
- 2 teaspoons cumin
- ¼ teaspoon dried sage
- 2 teaspoons crushed rosemary
- 1 tablespoon Worcestershire

For Injection:

- 1/8 teaspoon ground black pepper
- 1/8 teaspoon salt
- 1/8 teaspoon dried rosemary
- 1/2 teaspoon minced garlic
- 1/2 stick of salted butter, melted
- 1/2 teaspoon dried sage
- 2 teaspoons Worcestershire sauce
- Water as needed

Method:

1. Place all the ingredients for the rub in a bowl and stir until mixed.
2. Brush oil on all side of the roast, rub with the prepared spice mixture until evenly coated, then cover with plastic wrap and marinate in the refrigerator for 6 hours.
3. Then place all the ingredients for injection in a food processor and pulse for 1 minute or until grind.
4. Fill this mixture into injection and inject into marinated roast as deep as possible.
5. Cover roast again with plastic wrap and place in the refrigerator for 40 minutes.
6. Meanwhile, plug in the smoker, fill its tray with oak woodchips and water pan halfway through, and place dripping pan above the water pan.
7. Then open the top vent, shut with lid and use temperature settings to preheat smoker at 235 degrees F.
8. Place roast on smoker rack, place meat thermometer, then shut with lid smoke until meat thermometer registers an internal temperature of 140 degrees F.

9. Check vent of smoker every hour and add more woodchips and water to maintain temperature and smoke.
10. When done, wrap roast with aluminum foil and let rest for 20 minutes.
11. Then slice roast across the grain and serve.

Jalapeño Cheddar Beef Bombs

Servings: 8
Preparation time: 20 minutes
Cooking time: 2 hours

Nutrition Value:

Calories: 228 Cal, Carbs: 29 g, Fat: 6 g, Protein: 16 g, Fiber: 0 g.

Ingredients:

- 6 pounds ground beef
- 10 large jalapenos, diced
- 20 crackers, crushed
- 2 cups Italian bread crumbs
- 4 tablespoons onion powder
- 4 tablespoons garlic powder
- 3 tablespoons dried parsley
- 3 tablespoons salt
- 4 tablespoons ground black pepper
- 4 tablespoons dried oregano
- 3 tablespoons hot paprika
- 3-ounce Worcestershire sauce
- 2 cups milk, unsweetened
- 2 pounds cheddar cheese, shredded
- 6 eggs

Method:

1. Plug in the smoker, fill its tray with hickory woodchips and water pan halfway through, and place dripping pan above the water pan.
2. Then open the top vent, shut with lid and use temperature settings to preheat smoker at 225 degrees F.
3. In the meantime, place all the ingredients in a large bowl, stir until mixed and roll into balls.
4. Place balls on smoker rack, insert a meat thermometer, then shut with lid and smoke until meat thermometer registers an internal temperature of 165 degrees F.
5. Check vent of smoker every hour and add more woodchips and water to maintain temperature and smoke.
6. Serve straightaway.

Seasoned Chuck Roast

Servings: 12
Preparation time: 20 minutes
Cooking time: 6 hours

Nutrition Value:

Calories: 254 Cal, Carbs: 12.2 g, Fat: 9 g, Protein: 29.1 g, Fiber: 1.6 g.

Ingredients:

- 6 pounds chuck roast, boneless and fat trimmed
- 2 teaspoons onion powder
- 2 teaspoons garlic powder
- 1 ½ tablespoon sea salt
- 2 teaspoons ground black pepper
- 1 teaspoon brown sugar
- 1 teaspoon paprika
- 1/4 teaspoon cayenne

Method:

1. Rinse roast, pat dry using paper towels and place in a large baking dish.
2. Stir together remaining ingredients and rub this mixture on all sides of roast until evenly coated.
3. Then plug in the smoker, fill its tray with hickory woodchips and water pan halfway through, and place dripping pan above the water pan.
4. Then open the top vent, shut with lid and use temperature settings to preheat smoker at 250 degrees F.
5. Place roast on smoker rack, insert a meat thermometer, then shut with lid and set the timer to smoke for 6 hours or until meat thermometer register an internal temperature of 160 degrees F.
6. Check vent of smoker every hour and add more woodchips and water to maintain temperature and smoke.
7. Then wrap roast completely with aluminum foil and let sit for 1 hour.
8. Slice and serve roast as sandwiches.

Chapter9: Lamb

BBQ Lamb Chops

Servings: 4
Preparation time: 45 minutes
Cooking time: 2 hours and 30 minutes

Nutrition Value:

Calories: 235 Cal, Carbs: 0 g, Fat: 14 g, Protein: 25 g, Fiber: 0 g.

Ingredients:

- 4 lamb chops
- ½ teaspoon garlic powder
- 1 ½ teaspoon salt
- ½ teaspoon ground black pepper
- 1 tablespoon paprika
- 1 ½ teaspoon mustard powder
- ¼ cup apple cider vinegar
- ½ cup BBQ sauce

Method:

1. Pour vinegar in a large baking dish, add lamb chops and let soak for 30 minutes.
2. Then drain the chops and sprinkle with remaining ingredients except for BBQ sauce until evenly coated on all sides.
3. Plug in the smoker, fill its tray with mesquite woodchips and water pan halfway through, and place dripping pan above the water pan.
4. Then open the top vent, shut with lid and use temperature settings to preheat smoker at 225 degrees F.
5. Place chicken on smoker rack, place meat thermometer, then shut with lid and set the timer to smoke for 2 hours or more until meat thermometer register an internal temperature of 130 degrees F.
6. Check vent of smoker every hour and add more woodchips and water to maintain temperature and smoke.
7. Then brush BBQ sauce on all sides of lamb chops and continue smoking or until the internal temperature of lamb chops reach to 140 degrees F.
8. Serve straightaway.

Irish-Style Lamb

Servings: 6
Preparation time: 15 minutes
Cooking time: 4 hours

Nutrition Value:

Calories: 165 Cal, Carbs: 0 g, Fat: 11 g, Protein: 15 g, Fiber: 0 g.

Ingredients:

- 1 lamb leg, fat trimmed and boneless
- 2 teaspoons minced garlic
- 2 tablespoons salt
- 2 tablespoons ground black pepper
- 3 tablespoons rosemary, fresh

Method:

1. Plug in the smoker, fill its tray with hickory woodchips and water pan halfway through, and place dripping pan above the water pan.
2. Then open the top vent, shut with lid and use temperature settings to preheat smoker at 225 degrees F.
3. In the meantime, rinse leg of lamb, pat dry and then use a knife to butterfly its flesh.
4. Stir together remaining ingredients until combined, then place half of the spice mixture into the lamb, rub remaining spice mixture on all over the lamb and secure with kitchen twine.
5. Place leg of lamb on smoker rack, place meat thermometer, then shut with lid and set the timer to smoke for 4 hours or more until meat thermometer registers an internal temperature of 165 degrees F.
6. Check vent of smoker every hour and add more woodchips and water to maintain temperature and smoke.
7. Serve straightaway.

Lamb Barbacoa

Servings: 20
Preparation time: 15 minutes
Cooking time: 10 hours and 15 minutes

Nutrition Value:

Calories: 1000 Cal, Carbs: 19 g, Fat: 75 g, Protein: 60 g, Fiber: 0 g.

Ingredients:

- 10-pound leg of lamb, boneless
- Salsa verde for serving
- Sliced avocado for serving
- 12-ounce light beer

For Rub:

- 1 tablespoon cumin
- ½ teaspoon oregano, fresh
- ½ teaspoon coriander seed
- ½ teaspoon cinnamon
- ¼ teaspoon red chili powder
- 1 teaspoon salt
- ½ teaspoon ground black pepper

Method:

1. Plug in the smoker, fill its tray with hickory woodchips and water pan halfway through, and place dripping pan above the water pan.
2. Then open the top vent, shut with lid and use temperature settings to preheat smoker at 225 degrees F.
3. In the meantime, whisk together all the ingredients for rub until combined and then rub this mixture all over the leg of lamb until evenly coated.
4. Place leg of lamb on smoker rack, place meat thermometer, then shut with lid and set the timer to smoke for 8 to 10 hours or more until meat thermometer registers an internal temperature of 190 degrees F.
5. Check vent of smoker every hour and add more woodchips and water to maintain temperature and smoke.
6. When done, transfer leg of lamb on a cutting board, let rest for 15 minutes and then shred with a fork.
7. Place shredded lamb on a foil pan, pour in beer, stir until mixed and cover with aluminum foil.
8. Place the pan over low heat and steam until cooking liquid is reduced by half.
9. Serve lamb with salsa and avocado.

Smoked Lamb Shoulder

Servings: 16
Preparation time: 30 minutes
Cooking time: 5 hours

Nutrition Value:

Calories: 292 Cal, Carbs: 0 g, Fat: 21 g, Protein: 24.4 g, Fiber: 0 g.

Ingredients:

- 8 pounds lamb shoulder, fat trimmed
- 2 tablespoons olive oil

For Rub:

- 1 tablespoon dried thyme
- 1 tablespoon bay leaf
- 1 tablespoon dried oregano
- 2 tablespoons salt
- 2 tablespoons dried sage
- 1 tablespoon dried rosemary
- 1 tablespoon dried basil
- 1 tablespoon ground black pepper
- 1 tablespoon dried parsley
- 1 tablespoon sugar

Method:

1. Plug in the smoker, fill its tray with hickory woodchips and water pan halfway through, and place dripping pan above the water pan.
2. Then open the top vent, shut with lid and use temperature settings to preheat smoker at 250 degrees F.
3. In the meantime, rinse lamb, pat dry with paper towels and coat with oil.
4. Stir together all the ingredients for the rub and sprinkle on all sides of lamb until evenly coated.
5. Place lamb on smoker rack, fat-side up, insert a meat thermometer, then shut with lid and set the timer to smoke for 5 hours or more until meat thermometer registers an internal temperature of 300 degrees F.
6. Check vent of smoker every hour and add more woodchips and water to maintain temperature and smoke.
7. When done, cover the lamb with aluminum foil and let rest for 20 minutes.
8. Then shred lamb with a fork and serve.

Rosemary Lamb Chops

Servings: 12
Preparation time: 2 hours and 10 minutes
Cooking time: 50 minutes

Nutrition Value:

Calories: 171.5 Cal, Carbs: 0.4 g, Fat: 7.8 g, Protein: 23.2 g, Fiber: 0.1 g.

Ingredients:

- 12 lamb loin chops
- 3 teaspoons salt
- 1 tablespoon rosemary, chopped
- ¼ cup olive oil
- ¼ cup Jeff's rub

Method:

1. Sprinkle salt on top of chops and place in the refrigerator for 2 hours.
2. Meanwhile, stir together oil and rosemary and let sit for 1 hour.
3. After 2 hours, brush rosemary mixture on lamb chops and then sprinkle with the rub.
4. Plug in the smoker, fill its tray with hickory woodchips and water pan halfway through, and place dripping pan above the water pan.
5. Then open the top vent, shut with lid and use temperature settings to preheat smoker at 225 degrees F.
6. Place lamb chops on smoker rack, insert a meat thermometer, then shut with lid and set the timer to smoke for 50 minutes or more until meat thermometer registers an internal temperature of 165 degrees F.
7. When done, wrap lamb chops in aluminum foil for 10 minutes and then serve.

Smoked Rack of Lamb

Servings: 6
Preparation time: 3 hours and 25 minutes
Cooking time: 3 hours

Nutrition Value:

Calories: 335 Cal, Carbs: 2.4 g, Fat: 26.3 g, Protein: 21 g, Fiber: 0 g.

Ingredients:

- 1 rack of lamb, frenched

For Marinade:

- 2 tablespoons lemon juice
- 1/4 cup olive oil
- 2 tablespoons Dijon mustard
- 1 teaspoon dried rosemary, crushed
- ½ teaspoon ground black pepper
- 1 teaspoon minced garlic

For Rub:

- 1 teaspoon dried mint
- 1 teaspoon salt
- 1 teaspoon dried rosemary
- ¼ teaspoon cayenne pepper
- 1 teaspoon dried parsley
- 1 teaspoon garlic powder
- 1 tablespoon Dijon mustard
- 1 teaspoon dried oregano
- 1 teaspoon onion powder
- ¼ cup olive oil
- 1 teaspoon dried basil
- Balsamic reduction

Method:

1. Stir together all the ingredients for the marinade, then add into a large plastic bag, place rack of lamb in it, seal the bag and turn it upside down to evenly coat it.
2. Place the rack of lamb into the refrigerator to marinate for 2 to 3 hours.
3. Then remove the lamb from marinade, brush to coat lamb with mustard and sprinkle with garlic powder, onion powder, and cayenne pepper.
4. Stir together remaining ingredients of rub except for oil and balsamic reduction, then rub the spice mixture on all sides of lamb and drizzle with oil.
5. Plug in the smoker, fill its tray with hickory woodchips and water pan halfway through, and place dripping pan above the water pan.
6. Then open the top vent, shut with lid and use temperature settings to preheat smoker at 225 degrees F.

7. Place rack of lamb on smoker rack, insert a meat thermometer, then shut with lid and set the timer to smoke for 2 hours or more until meat thermometer registers an internal temperature of 145 degrees F.
8. Check vent of smoker every hour and add more woodchips and water to maintain temperature and smoke.
9. When done, cover the lamb with aluminum foil for 10 minutes, then slice and drizzle with balsamic reduction.
10. Serve straightaway.

Smoked Leg of Lamb

Servings: 8
Preparation time: 6 hours and 15 minutes
Cooking time: 5 hours

Nutrition Value:

Calories: 938 Cal, Carbs: 1.4 g, Fat: 69 g, Protein: 70.4 g, Fiber: 0.2 g.

Ingredients:

- 6 pounds leg of lamb
- 1 tablespoon minced garlic
- 1 teaspoon sea salt
- 1 teaspoon ground black pepper
- 1 teaspoon dried rosemary
- 1 teaspoon dried marjoram
- ½ cup wine vinegar
- ½ cup dry white wine
- ½ cup olive oil

Method:

1. Rinse lamb, pat dry with paper towels and place in a large plastic bag.
2. Place remaining ingredients in a blender, pulse for 1 minute or until smooth, then pour this mixture into the bag containing lamb and seal the bag.
3. Turn the plastic bag upside down to coat lamb with the spice mixture and then place in the refrigerator for 6 hours.
4. When ready to smoke, plug in the smoker, fill its tray with hickory woodchips and water pan halfway through, and place dripping pan above the water pan.
5. Then open the top vent, shut with lid and use temperature settings to preheat smoker at 225 degrees F.
6. In the meantime, remove the lamb from marinade and add marinade in the water pan of the smoker.
7. Place lamb on smoker rack, insert a meat thermometer, then shut with lid and set the timer to smoke for 4 to 5 hours or more until meat thermometer registers an internal temperature of 150 degrees F.
8. Check vent of smoker every hour and add more woodchips and water to maintain temperature and smoke.
9. Serve straightaway.

Smoked Lamb Lollipops

Servings: 4
Preparation time: 24 hours and 10 minutes
Cooking time: 1 hour

Nutrition Value:

Calories: 80 Cal, Carbs: 1 g, Fat: 6 g, Protein: 8 g, Fiber: 0 g.

Ingredients:

- 1 rack of lamb, fat trimmed
- 2 tablespoons shallots, peeled and chopped
- 1 teaspoon minced garlic
- ½ teaspoon salt
- ½ teaspoon ground black pepper
- 2 tablespoons rosemary, fresh
- 2 tablespoons sage, fresh
- 1 tablespoon thyme, fresh
- 1 tablespoon honey
- ¼ cup olive oil

Method:

1. Rinse lamb, pat dry and place in a baking dish.
2. Add remaining ingredients in a food processor, pulse for 1 minute or until smooth, then tip the mixture on lamb and rub well until evenly coated.
3. Cover dish with plastic wrap and marinate in the refrigerator for 24 hours.
4. When ready to smoke, plug in the smoker, fill its tray with hickory woodchips and water pan halfway through, and place dripping pan above the water pan.
5. Then open the top vent, shut with lid and use temperature settings to preheat smoker at 225 degrees F.
6. Place the marinated rack of lamb on smoker rack, insert a meat thermometer, then shut with lid and set the timer to smoke for 1 hour or more until meat thermometer registers an internal temperature of 120 degrees F.
7. When done, transfer lamb to a cutting board, let rest for 5 minutes and then slice to serve.

Smoked Lamb Breast

Servings: 6
Preparation time: 20 minutes
Cooking time: 2 hours and 30 minutes

Nutrition Value:

Calories: 230 Cal, Carbs: 0 g, Fat: 15 g, Protein: 24 g, Fiber: 0 g.

Ingredients:

- 2 pounds lamb breast, bone-in
- ½ cup apple cider vinegar
- ¼ cup yellow mustard
- ½ cup Barbecue Rub

Method:

1. Plug in the smoker, fill its tray with hickory woodchips and water pan halfway through, and place dripping pan above the water pan.
2. Then open the top vent, shut with lid and use temperature settings to preheat smoker at 250 degrees F.
3. In the meantime, rinse lamb with vinegar, then coat with mustard and sprinkle with BBQ rub.
4. Place lamb on smoker rack, insert a meat thermometer, then shut with lid and set the timer to smoke for 2 to 2 ½ hours or more until meat thermometer registers an internal temperature of 165 degrees F.
5. Check vent of smoker every hour and add more woodchips and water to maintain temperature and smoke.
6. When done, cover the lamb with aluminum foil and let rest for 10 minutes.
7. Slice to serve.

Boneless Leg of Lamb

Servings: 6
Preparation time: 1 hour and 15 minutes
Cooking time: 4 hours

Nutrition Value:

Calories: 213 Cal, Carbs: 1 g, Fat: 9 g, Protein: 29 g, Fiber: 0 g.

Ingredients:

- 2 ½ pounds leg of lamb, boneless and fat trimmed
- 2 teaspoons minced garlic
- 2 tablespoons salt
- 1 tablespoon ground black pepper
- 2 tablespoons oregano
- 1 teaspoon thyme
- 2 tablespoons olive oil

Method:

1. Rinse lamb, pat dry and place in a dish.
2. Stir together remaining ingredients until combined, then rub this spice mixture on all sides of lamb and cover the dish with plastic wrap.
3. Place dish into the refrigerator and marinate for 1 hour.
4. When ready to smoke, plug in the smoker, fill its tray with apple woodchips and water pan halfway through, and place dripping pan above the water pan.
5. Then open the top vent, shut with lid and use temperature settings to preheat smoker at 250 degrees F.
6. Place lamb on smoker rack, insert a meat thermometer, then shut with lid and set the timer to smoke for 3 to 4 hours or more until meat thermometer registers an internal temperature of 145 degrees F.
7. Check vent of smoker every hour and add more woodchips and water to maintain temperature and smoke.
8. Serve straightaway.

Chapter 10: Games

Smoked Rabbits

Servings: 6
Preparation time: 6 hours and 15 minutes
Cooking time: 1 hour and 30 minutes

Nutrition Value:

Calories: 167 Cal, Carbs: 0 g, Fat: 6.8 g, Protein: 24.7 g, Fiber: 0 g.

Ingredients:

- 1 whole rabbit, about 3 pounds
- 1 teaspoon minced garlic
- 1 teaspoon sea salt
- 2 teaspoons ground black pepper
- 1 tablespoon dried thyme
- 2 teaspoons dried oregano
- 1 tablespoon dried rosemary
- 1 bay leaf
- 1/3 cup olive oil
- 1/2 cup dry white wine

Method:

1. Rinse rabbit, pat dry and place in a large baking dish.
2. Stir together remaining ingredients, rub this mixture on all sides of rabbit, then wrap the dish with plastic wrap and refrigerate for 6 hours.
3. Then plug in the smoker, fill its tray with hickory woodchips and water pan halfway through, and place dripping pan above the water pan.
4. Then open the top vent, shut with lid and use temperature settings to preheat smoker at 240 degrees F.
5. In the meantime, bring the rabbit to room temperature.
6. Place rabbit on smoker rack, insert a meat thermometer, then shut with lid and set the timer to smoke for 1 hour and 30 minutes or more until meat thermometer registers an internal temperature of 165 degrees F, turning every 30 minutes.
7. Check vent of smoker every hour and add more woodchips and water to maintain temperature and smoke.
8. When done, wrap rabbit in aluminum foil, let rest for 15 minutes and carve into portions to serve.

Venison Jerky

Servings: 24
Preparation time: 8 hours and 5 minutes
Cooking time: 14 hours

Nutrition Value:

Calories: 35 Cal, Carbs: 2 g, Fat: 1 g, Protein: 6 g, Fiber: 0 g.

Ingredients:

- 8 pounds venison, ½ thick sliced
- ¼ cup salt
- ¼ teaspoon ground black pepper
- ½ teaspoon garlic salt
- ½ cup brown sugar
- ½ teaspoon dry mustard
- 1/8 cup Worcestershire sauce
- ½ cup soy sauce
- 3 cups water

Method:

1. Rinse venison, pat dry with paper towels and place in a large plastic bag.
2. Stir together remaining ingredients, add to venison, then seal the bag, turn it upside down to coat venison and let marinate for 8 hours.
3. Plug in the smoker, fill its tray with hickory woodchips and water pan halfway through, and place dripping pan above the water pan.
4. Then open the top vent, shut with lid and use temperature settings to preheat smoker at 140 degrees F.
5. Place venison on smoker rack, place meat thermometer, then shut with lid and set the timer to smoke for 16 hours.
6. Check vent of smoker every hour and add more woodchips and water to maintain temperature and smoke.
7. Serve straightaway.

Smoked Venison Tenderloin

Servings: 2
Preparation time: 12 hours and 30 minutes
Cooking time: 2 hours

Nutrition Value:

Calories: 33 Cal, Carbs: 0 g, Fat: 1 g, Protein: 6 g, Fiber: 0 g.

Ingredients:

- 2 venison tenderloins, each about 8 ounces
- ½ of small white onion, peeled and diced
- 1 teaspoon minced garlic
- 1 teaspoon sea salt
- 1 teaspoon ground black pepper
- 1 teaspoon dried rosemary
- 1 teaspoon honey
- 1 teaspoon Dijon mustard
- 1/4 cup olive oil
- 1/3 cup dry red wine
- 1 tablespoon soy sauce

Method:

1. Rinse venison, pat dry and place in a large plastic bag.
2. Stir together remaining ingredients until combined, add into venison, then seal the bag and turn it upside down to coat venison until evenly coated.
3. Then place bag into the refrigerator for 12 hours or until marinated.
4. Plug in the smoker, fill its tray with hickory woodchips and water pan halfway through, and place dripping pan above the water pan.
5. Then open the top vent, shut with lid and use temperature settings to preheat smoker at 250 degrees F.
6. In the meantime, remove venison from the marinade and bring to room temperature.
7. Place venison on smoker rack, insert meat thermometer, then shut with lid and set the timer to smoke for 2 hours or more until meat thermometer register an internal temperature of 150 degrees F.
8. Check vent of smoker every hour and add more woodchips and water to maintain temperature and smoke.
9. When done, wrap venison in aluminum foil, let rest for 20 minutes and slice thinly to serve.

Boar Shoulder

Servings: 12
Preparation time: 8 hours and 30 minutes
Cooking time: 4 hours

Nutrition Value:

Calories: 35 Cal, Carbs: 0 g, Fat: 1 g, Protein: 6.1 g, Fiber: 0 g.

Ingredients:

- 6-pound boar shoulder roast
- 3/4 cup salt
- 2 tablespoons ground black pepper
- 1 cup brown sugar
- 1 tablespoon dried rosemary
- 2 whole bay leaves
- 1/4 cup Worcestershire sauce
- 1/2 cup of soy sauce
- 1-gallon water

Method:

1. Place a large pot over medium heat, pour in water and bring to boil.
2. Remove pot from heat, add salt and sugar, stir until dissolved and set aside until cooled.
3. Then remaining ingredients except for boar, stir until mixed and pour the mixture into a large bag.
4. Add boar, seal the bag and place in the refrigerator for 8 hours.
5. Plug in the smoker, fill its tray with hickory woodchips and water pan halfway through, and place dripping pan above the water pan.
6. Then open the top vent, shut with lid and use temperature settings to preheat smoker at 275 degrees F.
7. In the meantime, remove boar from the marinade and bring to room temperature.
8. Place boar on smoker rack, insert a meat thermometer, then shut with lid and set the timer to smoke for 4 hours or more until meat thermometer registers an internal temperature of 155 degrees F.
9. Check vent of smoker every hour and add more woodchips and water to maintain temperature and smoke.
10. When done, wrap boar in aluminum foil, let rest for 20 minutes and slice thinly to serve.

Smoked Pheasant

Servings: 2
Preparation time: 10 hours and 30 minutes
Cooking time: 5 hours

Nutrition Value:

Calories: 242 Cal, Carbs: 0 g, Fat: 6 g, Protein: 44 g, Fiber: 0 g.

Ingredients:

- 2 whole pheasants with skin on, each about 2 pounds
- 1/2 cup salt
- 1/2 teaspoon ground black pepper
- 1/2 cup brown sugar
- 1 tsp dried thyme
- 1/2 teaspoon dried sage
- 1 bay leaf
- 1 cup honey
- ½ lemon, juiced
- 8 cups water

Method:

1. Place a large pot over medium heat, pour in water, bring to boil and then stir in salt and sugar.
2. Remove pot from heat and set aside until cooked.
3. Add black pepper, thyme, sage, and bay leaf, stir until combined, then add pheasants, cover the pot and let soak in the refrigerator for 8 to 10 hours.
4. Then rinse pheasant, pat dry with paper towels, place them in a sheet pan and refrigerate for 2 hours or until dry.
5. After 2 hours, bring pheasant's temperature to room temperature, then tie its legs with kitchen twine and tuck them under the wings.
6. Meanwhile, plug in the smoker, fill its tray with hickory woodchips and water pan halfway through, and place dripping pan above the water pan.
7. Then open the top vent, shut with lid and use temperature settings to preheat smoker at 250 degrees F.
8. Place pheasants on smoker rack, insert a meat thermometer, then shut with lid and set the timer to smoke for 3 to 5 hours or more until meat thermometer registers an internal temperature of 165 degrees F.
9. Meanwhile, stir together honey and lemon juice in a saucepan and cook over low heat until heated through and then baste pheasants with this mixture every hour.
10. When done, wrap pheasants with aluminum foil and let rest for 10 minutes before serving.

Bacon Wrapped Dove

Servings: 4
Preparation time: 15 minutes
Cooking time: 1 hour

Nutrition Value:

Calories: 524 Cal, Carbs: 1 g, Fat: 51 g, Protein: 13 g, Fiber: 0 g.

Ingredients:

- 4 dove breasts, cleaned
- 4 slices of bacon
- 4 slices of mushrooms, each ¼-inch thick
- 1 teaspoon ground black pepper

Method:

1. Plug in the smoker, fill its tray with apple woodchips and water pan halfway through, and place dripping pan above the water pan.
2. Then open the top vent, shut with lid and use temperature settings to preheat smoker at 225 degrees F.
3. In the meantime, season dove with black pepper, then wrap each dove with a slice of bacon and secure with a skewer.
4. Place dove on smoker rack, place meat thermometer, then shut with lid and set the timer to smoke for 1 hour or more until meat thermometer register an internal temperature of 165 degrees F.
5. Serve straightaway.

Whole Quail

Servings: 6
Preparation time: 6 hours and 20 minutes
Cooking time: 3 hours

Nutrition Value:

Calories: 175 Cal, Carbs: 0 g, Fat: 9 g, Protein: 22 g, Fiber: 0 g.

Ingredients:

- 6 whole quail, skin on
- 1 apple, cored and cut into 6 equal pieces
- 1 teaspoon garlic powder
- 2 teaspoons sea salt
- 1 teaspoon ground black pepper
- 1 teaspoon smoky paprika
- 1/2 teaspoon dried thyme
- 1/2 teaspoon dried oregano
- 1/4 of lemon, zested
- 2 1/2 tablespoons olive oil

Method:

1. Rinse quail, pat dry and place in a large baking dish.
2. Stir together remaining ingredients and rub the mixture all over the quail until evenly coated.
3. Then cover the dish with a plastic wrap and place in the refrigerator for 4 to 6 hours.
4. Plug in the smoker, fill its tray with hickory woodchips and water pan halfway through, and place dripping pan above the water pan.
5. Then open the top vent, shut with lid and use temperature settings to preheat smoker at 220 degrees F.
6. In the meantime, remove quail from the refrigerator and bring its temperature to room temperature.
7. Place quail on smoker rack, insert a meat thermometer, then shut with lid and set the timer to smoke for 3 hours or more until meat thermometer registers an internal temperature of 145 degrees F.
8. Check vent of smoker every hour and add more woodchips and water to maintain temperature and smoke.
9. When done, wrap quail in aluminum foil, let rest for 15 minutes and serve.

Smoked Veal

Servings: 8
Preparation time: 4 hours and 20 minutes
Cooking time: 3 hours

Nutrition Value:

Calories: 514 Cal, Carbs: 0 g, Fat: 22.6 g, Protein: 73 g, Fiber: 0 g.

Ingredients:

- 1-pound veal loin roast
- 3 oranges, zested
- 2 limes, zested
- 1 tablespoon chopped ginger
- 2 teaspoons chopped chilis
- 1 teaspoon salt
- ½ teaspoon ground black pepper
- 1 teaspoon cinnamon
- ½ teaspoon nutmeg
- ¼ cup olive oil

Method:

1. Rinse veal, pat dry with paper towels and place in a large plastic bag.
2. Stir together remaining ingredients, add to venison, seal the bag, then turn it upside down to coat venison and place in the refrigerator for 4 hours.
3. Plug in the smoker, fill its tray with hickory woodchips and water pan halfway through, and place dripping pan above the water pan.
4. Then open the top vent, shut with lid and use temperature settings to preheat smoker at 220 degrees F.
5. Place venison on smoker rack, insert a meat thermometer, then shut with lid and set the timer to smoke for 3 hours or more until meat thermometer registers an internal temperature of 165 degrees F.
6. Check vent of smoker every hour and add more woodchips and water to maintain temperature and smoke.
7. When done, wrap venison in aluminum foil for 15 minutes and then slice to serve.

Smoked Duck

Servings: 1
Preparation time: 4 hours and 20 minutes
Cooking time: 4 hours

Nutrition Value:

Calories: 472 Cal, Carbs: 0 g, Fat: 40 g, Protein: 27 g, Fiber: 0 g.

Ingredients:

- 1 whole duck, each about 6 pounds
- 2 tablespoons garlic salt
- 2 tablespoons ground black pepper
- ¾ cup honey
- ¾ cup soy sauce
- ¾ cup red wine vinegar

Method:

1. Rinse duck, pat dry with paper towels and place in a large plastic bag.
2. Stir together remaining ingredients, add to duck, then seal the bag, turn it upside down to coat duck and place in the refrigerator for 4 hours.
3. Plug in the smoker, fill its tray with hickory woodchips and water pan halfway through, and place dripping pan above the water pan.
4. Then open the top vent, shut with lid and use temperature settings to preheat smoker at 250 degrees F.
5. Place duck on smoker rack, place meat thermometer, then shut with lid and set the timer to smoke for 1 hour.
6. Then baste the duck with marinade and smoke for 3 hours or until meat thermometer register an internal temperature of 165 degrees F
7. Check vent of smoker every hour and add more woodchips and water to maintain temperature and smoke.
8. Serve straightaway.

Cornish Game Hens

Servings: 8
Preparation time: 1 hour
Cooking time: 2 hours and 30 minutes

Nutrition Value:

Calories: 331 Cal, Carbs: 0 g, Fat: 9.6 g, Protein: 57.7 g, Fiber: 0 g.

Ingredients:

- 4 whole Cornish game hens
- 3 oranges, cut into quarters
- 4 teaspoons sea salt
- 2 teaspoons ground black pepper
- 2 teaspoons dried thyme
- 1/4 cup olive oil

Method:

1. Rinse hens, pat dry with paper towels and let rest for 30 minutes at room temperature.
2. Then plug in the smoker, fill its tray with hickory woodchips and water pan halfway through, and place dripping pan above the water pan.
3. Then open the top vent, shut with lid and use temperature settings to preheat smoker at 250 degrees F.
4. In the meantime, stir together remaining ingredients except for oranges and rub on all sides of hens until evenly coated.
5. Stuff each hen with 3 quarters of hen and tie the legs with kitchen twine.
6. Place hens on smoker rack, place meat thermometer, then shut with lid and set the timer to smoke for 2 hours and 30 minutes or more until meat thermometer registers an internal temperature of 165 degrees F.
7. Check vent of smoker every hour and add more woodchips and water to maintain temperature and smoke.
8. When done, wrap hens with aluminum foil for 20 minutes, then cut each hen into half and serve.

Chapter 11: Sides

Smoked Artichokes

Servings: 4
Preparation time: 10 minutes
Cooking time: 1 hour

Nutrition Value:

Calories: 15 Cal, Carbs: 0.7 g, Fat: 1.3 g, Protein: 0.5 g, Fiber: 1 g.

Ingredients:

- 4 whole artichokes, halved
- 4 minced garlic
- ¾ teaspoon sea salt
- ½ teaspoon ground black pepper
- 1 lemon, juiced
- ½ cup olive oil

Method:

1. Plug in the smoker, fill its tray with hickory woodchips and water pan halfway through, and place dripping pan above the water pan.
2. Then open the top vent, shut with lid and use temperature settings to preheat smoker at 200 degrees F.
3. In the meantime, place artichokes in a foil pan, then add remaining ingredients and stir well until evenly coated.
4. Place foil pan containing artichokes on smoker rack, then shut with lid and set the timer to smoke for 1 hour.
5. Serve straightaway.

Smoked Asparagus and Onion Mix

Servings: 4
Preparation time: 10 minutes
Cooking time: 2 hours

Nutrition Value:

Calories: 45 Cal, Carbs: 4 g, Fat: 3 g, Protein: 2.2 g, Fiber: 1.9 g.

Ingredients:

- 1 ½ pound asparagus
- 1 medium white onion, peeled and sliced
- 1 ½ teaspoon salt
- ¼ teaspoon ground black pepper
- 2 tablespoons lemon juice

Method:

1. Plug in the smoker, fill its tray with hickory woodchips and water pan halfway through, and place dripping pan above the water pan.
2. Then open the top vent, shut with lid and use temperature settings to preheat smoker at 225 degrees F.
3. In the meantime, spread onion on the bottom on foil pan, then top with asparagus, season with salt and black pepper and drizzle with lemon juice.
4. Place pan containing asparagus on smoker rack, then shut with lid and set the timer to smoke for 2 hours.
5. Check vent of smoker every hour and add more woodchips and water to maintain temperature and smoke.
6. Serve straightaway.

Smoked Guacamole

Servings: 6
Preparation time: 40 minutes
Cooking time: 40 minutes

Nutrition Value:

Calories: 352 Cal, Carbs: 20 g, Fat: 32 g, Protein: 4.2 g, Fiber: 14 g.

Ingredients:

- 6 medium avocados
- 4 Roma tomatoes, cored and sliced
- 1 bunch of fresh cilantros, chopped
- 1 small white onion, peeled and halved
- 1 teaspoon minced garlic
- 1 teaspoon salt
- ½ teaspoon ground black pepper
- 2 limes, juiced and zested

Method:

1. Plug in the smoker, fill its tray with apple woodchips and water pan halfway through, and place dripping pan above the water pan.
2. Then open the top vent, shut with lid and use temperature settings to preheat smoker at 275 degrees F.
3. In the meantime, place tomatoes and onions on a foil pan.
4. Place pan containing onion and tomatoes on smoker rack, then shut with lid and set the timer to smoke for 40 minutes.
5. When done, remove the pan from smoker, cool vegetables completely and chop roughly.
6. Meanwhile, cut avocado into half, remove is seed and scoop the flesh into a bowl.
7. Season with salt, black pepper, lime zest and juice and mash with a fork until smooth.
8. Add smokes tomatoes and onions along with remaining ingredients and stir until mixed.
9. Cover the bowl with plastic wrap and let chill for 30 minutes in the refrigerator.
10. Serve guacamole with corn chips.

Smoked Cauliflower

Servings: 4
Preparation time: 10 minutes
Cooking time: 2 hours

Nutrition Value:

Calories: 107 Cal, Carbs: 6.2 g, Fat: 8.9 g, Protein: 2.5 g, Fiber: 3.1 g.

Ingredients:

- 1 whole cauliflower
- 1 ¼ teaspoon salt
- ¾ teaspoon ground black pepper
- ½ teaspoon dried oregano
- 2 tablespoons olive oil
- ½ teaspoon dried basil

Method:

1. Plug in the smoker, fill its tray with hickory woodchips and water pan halfway through, and place dripping pan above the water pan.
2. Then open the top vent, shut with lid and use temperature settings to preheat smoker at 200 degrees F.
3. In the meantime, cut cauliflower into florets, then place into a foil pan, add remaining ingredients and toss until well mixed.
4. Place pan containing cauliflower florets on smoker rack, then shut with lid and set the timer to smoke for 2 hours.
5. Check vent of smoker every hour and add more woodchips and water to maintain temperature and smoke.
6. Serve straightaway.

Corn on Cob

Servings: 12
Preparation time: 2 hours and 10 minutes
Cooking time: 2 hours

Nutrition Value:

Calories: 58 Cal, Carbs: 14.1 g, Fat: 0.5 g, Protein: 2 g, Fiber: 1.8 g.

Ingredients:

- 12 ears of corn
- 3 teaspoon salt
- 1 ½ teaspoon ground black pepper
- 3 tablespoons unsalted butter
- Water as needed

Method:

1. Peel the husk to the stem from each corn, then place it over the ears of corn and soak in water for 2 hours in a large container.
2. Plug in the smoker, fill its tray with oak woodchips and water pan halfway through, and place dripping pan above the water pan.
3. Then open the top vent, shut with lid and use temperature settings to preheat smoker at 225 degrees F.
4. In the meantime,
5. Place corn on smoker rack, then shut with lid and set the timer to smoke for 2 hours.
6. Check vent of smoker every hour and add more woodchips and water to maintain temperature and smoke.
7. When done, drizzle butter all over the corn, then season with salt and black pepper and serve.

Smoked Portobello Mushrooms

Servings: 6
Preparation time: 10 minutes
Cooking time: 2 hours

Nutrition Value:

Calories: 15 Cal, Carbs: 2.2 g, Fat: 0.3 g, Protein: 1.7 g, Fiber: 1.1 g.

Ingredients:

- 12 large Portobello mushrooms, de-stemmed
- 2 ½ teaspoons sea salt
- 1 ½ teaspoon ground black pepper
- 2 teaspoons Herbs de Provence
- 4 tablespoons olive oil

Method:

1. Plug in the smoker, fill its tray with hickory woodchips and water pan halfway through, and place dripping pan above the water pan.
2. Then open the top vent, shut with lid and use temperature settings to preheat smoker at 200 degrees F.
3. In the meantime, rinse mushrooms, pat dry with paper towels, then place in a foil pan cap-side down, drizzle with oil and season with salt, black pepper, and herbs de Provence.
4. Place pan containing mushrooms on smoker rack, then shut with lid and set the timer to smoke for 2 hours.
5. Check vent of smoker every hour and add more woodchips and water to maintain temperature and smoke.
6. Serve straightaway.

Smoked Eggplant and Baba Ghanoush

Servings: 4
Preparation time: 10 minutes
Cooking time: 1 hour

Nutrition Value:

Calories: 116 Cal, Carbs: 8 g, Fat: 8 g, Protein: 3 g, Fiber: 2.3 g.

Ingredients:

- 2 medium eggplants
- ½ teaspoon minced garlic
- 1 teaspoon sea salt
- 1/2 teaspoon ground black pepper
- 4 tablespoons tahini
- 3 tablespoons lemon juice
- 2 teaspoons olive oil and more for brushing

Method:

1. Plug in the smoker, fill its tray with hickory woodchips and water pan halfway through, and place dripping pan above the water pan.
2. Then open the top vent, shut with lid and use temperature settings to preheat smoker at 200 degrees F.
3. In the meantime, cut eggplants into ¼-inch slices, then coat with olive oil and place on a foil pan.
4. Place pan containing eggplant on smoker rack, then shut with lid and set the timer to smoke for 1 hour or until soft.
5. When done, let the eggplant cool for 15 minutes, then add to a food processor along with remaining ingredients and pulse for 1 to 2 minutes or until creamy.
6. Garnish with parsley and serve with pita bread.

Smoked Cabbage

Servings: 3
Preparation time: 10 minutes
Cooking time: 2 hours

Nutrition Value:

Calories: 87 Cal, Carbs: 8.2 g, Fat: 6.2 g, Protein: 1.8 g, Fiber: 2.7 g.

Ingredients:

- 1 small head of green cabbage
- 1/2 teaspoon sea salt and more as needed
- 1/2 teaspoon ground black pepper and more as needed
- 1 tablespoon apple cider vinegar
- 2 tablespoons butter
- 2 tablespoons olive oil

Method:

1. Plug in the smoker, fill its tray with hickory woodchips and water pan halfway through, and place dripping pan above the water pan.
2. Then open the top vent, shut with lid and use temperature settings to preheat smoker at 225 degrees F.
3. In the meantime, remove the core of cabbage, then fill it with vinegar, season with salt and black pepper and rub with butter.
4. Season exterior of cabbage with salt and black pepper and place it in a foil pan.
5. Place cabbage on smoker rack, then shut with lid and set the timer to smoke for 1 hour and 30 minutes.
6. Check vent of smoker every hour and add more woodchips and water to maintain temperature and smoke.
7. Then smoke cabbage directly in the smoker for 30 minutes and then cut into wedges to serve.

Smoked Sweet Onions

Servings: 6
Preparation time: 10 minutes
Cooking time: 3 hours

Nutrition Value:

Calories: 9 Cal, Carbs: 2.14 g, Fat: 0.02 g, Protein: 0.23 g, Fiber: 0.3 g.

Ingredients:

- 6 large sweet onions, peeled and de-stemmed
- 2 teaspoons ginger powder
- 1 teaspoon sea salt
- 1 teaspoon ground black pepper
- 2 teaspoons red chili powder
- 2 teaspoons allspice
- 2 teaspoons dried thyme
- 3 tablespoons olive oil

Method:

1. Plug in the smoker, fill its tray with hickory woodchips and water pan halfway through, and place dripping pan above the water pan.
2. Then open the top vent, shut with lid and use temperature settings to preheat smoker at 200 degrees F.
3. In the meantime, stir together all the ingredients except for onions until combined and then brush all over the onions.
4. Place onions on smoker rack, then shut with lid and set the timer to smoke for 3 hours or until done.
5. Check vent of smoker every hour and add more woodchips and water to maintain temperature and smoke.
6. Slice onions and serve.

Smoked Potatoes

Servings: 6
Preparation time: 10 minutes
Cooking time: 2 hours

Nutrition Value:

Calories: 42 Cal, Carbs: 7.3 g, Fat: 1.3 g, Protein: 0.8 g, Fiber: 0.5 g.

Ingredients:

- 6 medium potatoes, rinsed
- 2 teaspoons sea salt
- 1 teaspoon ground black pepper
- ¼ cup olive oil

Method:

1. Plug in the smoker, fill its tray with hickory woodchips and water pan halfway through, and place dripping pan above the water pan.
2. Then open the top vent, shut with lid and use temperature settings to preheat smoker at 225 degrees F.
3. In the meantime, pork potato with a fork, then brushes with olive oil and season with salt and black pepper.
4. Place potatoes on smoker rack, then shut with lid and set the timer to smoke for 2 hours, turning halfway through.
5. Check vent of smoker every hour and add more woodchips and water to maintain temperature and smoke.
6. Serve potatoes with butter and sour cream.

Conclusion

The Masterbuilt Electric Smoker is one of the best innovations for people who loves smoked food as it has made smoked meals much easier and quicker. Now you can easily smoke your favorite meat and enjoy it quickly.

In this book, there are many carefully selected recipes that are bound to help you delight all your family and friends with the best and most popular smoker dishes. Masterbuilt Electric Smoker Cookbook 2021 will help you keep the culinary tradition of smoke cooking alive and will remind you that smoking food is one of the most ancient and most cherished cooking traditions that will help you enjoy food the way you never enjoyed before!

CPSIA information can be obtained
at www.ICGtesting.com
Printed in the USA
BVHW011519161221
624022BV00019B/286